THE **NEAL-SCHUMAN** INDEX TO

SPORTS FIGURES

IN COLLECTIVE BIOGRAPHIES

COMPILED BY
PAULETTE BOCHNIG SHARKEY

NEAL-SCHUMAN INDEX SERIES
JIM ROGINSKI, SERIES EDITOR

NEAL-SCHUMAN PUBLISHERS, INC.
NEW YORK   LONDON

Published by Neal-Schuman Publishers, Inc.
23 Leonard Street
New York, New York 10013

Printed and bound in the United States of America.

Library of Congress Cataloging-in-Publication Data

Sharkey, Paulette Bochnig.
    The Neal-Schuman index to sports figures in collective biographies
/ compiled by Paulette Bochnig Sharkey.
        p.   cm. — (Neal-Schuman indexes series : 2)
    Includes bibliographical references.
    ISBN 1-55570-055-1
    1. Athletes—Biography—Indexes. I. Title. II. Title: Index to
sports figures in collective biographies. III. Series.
GV697.A1S475   1991
796'.092'2—dc20
[B]   90-30605
                                                        CIP

To J.S.B.S.

Table of Contents

Acknowledgments, vii

To the Librarian, ix

To the Student, xi

Key to Symbols, xiv

Main Entries, 3

Index to Sports Figures by Sport, 113

Index to Women Sports Figures, 130

Index to Sports Figures by Country of Origin, 133

Bibliography and Book Codes, 150

Acknowledgments

This index would not have been possible without the excellent resources of the Madison [Wisconsin] Public Library and the help of its Interlibrary Loan department. The ILL staff handled countless requests for material and if they tired of it, they never let me know. A special thanks is due to the gracious staff of the Monroe Street Branch, especially Dorothy Batt, whose enthusiasm for the project kept me going. It was also a pleasure to work with Jim Roginski in creating this index. He provided thoughtful advice, a level-headed approach, and a terrific sense of humor. And I'm grateful to my husband, Tom Sharkey, for solving many computer problems and, as usual, for helping me keep it all in perspective.

PMBS

For my part, to Pat Schuman for her willingness to take a gamble; Barry and Neal for counting; and Barry, again, for being a who's who of wrestlers and wrestling; and, of course, Paulette, for compiling this index and helping to develop the correct format for it.

JR

To the Librarian

The Neal-Schuman Index to Sports Figures inaugurates a series of occasional reference books designed for easy use by children and young adults for which minimal assistance is required from a librarian or teacher. Indexes in the series are based on literature published for children and young adults and are designed to answer personal or school-related questions more quickly as well as to reinforce the need for successful (and continuing) library skills on the part of the student. You will want to refer students to pages xi-xiv, To the Student, for understanding how this index works.

Criteria: Individual collective biographies published for children and young adults indexed here were published between 1970 and 1988. A total of 255 collective biographies have been indexed. Individual biographies, autobiographies and reference books with a "who's who" type entry have not been included.

Entries: There are 1,670 individual name entries here, representing historical and contemporary sports figures. Most entries are listed by nicknames or informal names with birthnames following in parentheses. The premise is that children and young adults are more likely to ask for material about "Dizzy Dean" than "J. Hanna Dean."

Indexes: Three comprehensive indexes are included: by sport category [34 entries], women athletes [177 entries, which are also incorporated in the sports index], and by country of origin [45 entries].

Names and Dates: Every reasonable effort was made to provide correct birthnames and birthdates. When information was lacking in the collective biographies themselves, standard sports reference books as well as general and specialized biographical sources were searched. Extensive use was made of information found in editions of the *Official Encyclopedia of Baseball* (A. S. Barnes), *Biographical Dictionary of American Sports* series (Greenwood Press), and the *Biography and Genealogy Master Index* (Gale Research).

INDEX TO SPORTS FIGURES

Cross References: See references to main listings have been incorporated when necessary for legally changed names, nicknames, or names changed by marriage.

Subject Headings: Subject headings for the individual sports are from the *Sears List of Subject Headings*, with slight modifications to allow for easier use. An occasional sports figure who is not an athlete is identified as such in the main entries. These categories include "commissioner," "owner," "manager," "promoter," or "umpire."

Key to Symbols: Please see page xiv for an explanation of these.

Bibliography and Book Codes: See page 150 for these. Those books which have been recommended by the *Children's Catalog, Elementary School Library Collection, Junior High School Library Catalog, Public Library Catalog*, and *Senior High School Library Catalog* are so noted.

We are very interested in your reaction to the concept of this book and its success with your library patrons. We invite your ideas for further development of the series. Please send any comments you may have to me at Neal-Schuman Publishers, 23 Leonard Street, New York, NY 10013.

Jim Roginski
Series Editor

To the Student

The purpose of this index is to help you find information about individual athletes in collective biographies. Collective biographies are books about two or more people. The athletes are entered by last name or nickname in alphabetical order. Last names beginning with "Mc" or "Mac" are alphabetized as if they are spelled "Mac." If a name includes "Dr." or "Mr.", it's alphabetized as if it is spelled "Doctor" or "Mister."

To use this book, follow the simple steps below.

1. Find the athlete by nickname or last name, a changed name [such as Kareem Abdul-Jabbar], or in the case of an married woman, her maiden name. Thus:

Evert, Chris.

2. If an athlete is listed by a nickname, and if the name the athlete was born with is known, the second part of the entry looks like:

[b. Henry Lewis.]

(birthname; "b" means born; a listing without capital letters means the athlete's last name did not change)

With capital letters, the entry will look like:

[b. Henry Lewis FORD.]

(full birthname; capital letters indicate the full name the athlete was born with and means that his or her last name was changed later on)

Sometimes sports figures are known very well by their real names and nicknames, so the entry looks like:

[also known as Wilt the Stilt].

For women athletes only, you will see:

[m. Johnson].

INDEX TO SPORTS FIGURES

(tells you this woman athlete married someone with the last name of Johnson)

    3. The third section tells you the year the athlete was born:

        1903- .

(born in 1903 and still alive)

Or:

        Birthdate?

(unclear when the athlete was born, and may or may not be living)

        ?-1961.

(unclear when the athlete was born, but did die in 1961)

        1903?- .

(athlete may have been born in 1903 and is still alive)

        1903?-1961.

(athlete may have been born in 1903, but did die in 1961)

        1903-1961.

(athlete was born in 1903 and died in 1961)

    4. Fourth, is the country the athlete was born in:

        United States.

Or:

        United States?

(unclear if the athlete is from the United States or not)

    5. Fifth, the entry tells you the sport the athlete is or was well known in:

        Wrestling.

Or:

        Football and Soccer.

(if the athlete was known in two or more sports)

Or:

        Wrestling [manager].

(officials who work with athletes; also: "commissioner," "manager," "owner," "promoter," "sports announcer," or "umpire"

6. Sometimes you will see a listing like:

Alcindor, Ferdinand Lewis Jr. *see* Abdul-Jabbar, Kareem

Or:

Buzonas, Gail Johnson *see* Johnson, Gail

Or:

Roussimoff, Andrae Rene *see* André the Giant

These are called cross-references or "see" references. They tell you exactly where to find the person you're looking for in this book.

In the examples here, Kareem Abdul-Jabbar was born Ferdinand Lewis Alcindor, Jr., but because he is better known as Kareem Abdul-Jabbar, he is listed under Abdul-Jabbar, Kareem. Gail Johnson, who is known under her married name, Gail Johnson Buzonas, is listed under Gail Johnson, because that is the name she is known by as an athlete. "André the Giant" is listed under his wrestling name because few people know him by his real name, Andrae Rene Roussimoff.

Key to Symbols

Following each main entry is a coded list which tells you what books have information about the athlete. Other symbols tell how much information you'll find in the book and whether photographs or drawings are included. For example:

AHRK **
ASHT ** p
BFAM * i
CHMP ** i/c
FSWS **** p, i
HITT ** p, p/c

You will find the full description of the book codes on pages 150-167 of this book.

The symbols mean:

*	less than one page of information
**	1-10 pages of information
***	11-25 pages of information
****	more than 25 pages of information
p	black and white photograph[s]
p/c	color photograph[s]
i	black and white drawing[s] or illustration[s]
i/c	color drawing[s] or illustration[s]

Once you have the titles of the books you need, check your library catalog to see which books your library owns. Then check your library shelves. If your library does not have the books you need, ask your librarian to help you to get your books from another library. This is called "Interlibrary Loan."

Starting on page 113, you will find athletes indexed by their sport. A separate index lists all the women athletes in this book, beginning on page 130. On page 133 is an index to athletes by the countries in which they were born. Page numbers telling you where to find the athletes in this book follow each listing.

Part One
Main Entries

Aaron, Hank. [b. Henry Lewis].
1934-   . United States.
Baseball.
    AHRK **
    ASHT ** p
    BATA ** p
    BEYD **
    BFAM * i
    BGSL *** p
    BHRH ** p
    BIBA ***
    BOBG ** p
    CHMP ** i/c
    FSWS **** p, i
    GBST ** p
    HITT ** p, p/c
    HUNB ** p
    MOBS *** p
    RBML ** p
    SMAA **
    SPIM ** p
    TSBG ** p

Abdul-Jabbar, Kareem. [b.
Ferdinand Lewis ALCINDOR,
Jr.]. 1947-   . United States.
Basketball.
    ASHT ** p
    BBGM ** p
    CENT ** p/c
    CHMP ** p/c, i/c
    FSWS **** p, i
    HSPB *** p
    LONH *** p
    MBBS *** p
    PBBM **** p
    PBGR ***
    RBPS ** p
    ROOK **** p
    SOPB ** p
    SPIM ** p

Abramowicz, Danny. [b. Daniel].
1945-   . United States. Football.
    SPRN *** p

Albano, Captain Lou. Birthdate?
United States. Wrestling.
    WRE2 ** p

Albright, Tenley Emma. 1935-   .
United States. Ice Skating.
    AOGL *** p
    AWIS ** p
    GLTR ** p
    GOLG ** p
    HUNW ** p
    WSFS *

Alcindor, Ferdinand Lewis Jr.
see Abdul-Jabbar, Kareem

Alexander, Pete. [b. Grover
Cleveland]. 1887-1950. United
States. Baseball.
    BATA ** p
    HOFB ** p
    HUNB ** p

Ali, Muhammad. [b. Cassius
Marcellus CLAY, Jr.]. 1942-   .
United States. Boxing.
    AOGL *** p
    ASHT ** p
    BEYD **
    BHCF ** p, p/c
    BHWC ** p
    CHCH **
    GCIS ** p
    GRLS ** p
    HWCH *** p
    POBS ** p
    RCHN **
    SFST ** p

SPIM ** p
TDTL *** p
WUND *** p

Allen, Dick. [b. Richard
Anthony]. 1942- . United
States. Baseball.
HHCR ** p
MOBS ** p

Allen, George. 1922- . United
States. Football.
COAH ** p, p/c
COAL ** p
FOCC ** p

Allen, Lisa-Marie. 1961?- .
United States. Ice Skating.
STOI ** p

Allen, Marcus. 1960- . United
States. Football.
HATG **

Allison, Bobby. [b. Robert
Arthur]. 1937- . United States.
Automobile Racing.
DOSW * p
HSCR ** p
MARS *** p

Almon, Bill. [b. William Francis].
1952- . United States.
Baseball.
BPTH *** p

Alou, Felipe Rojas. 1935- .
Dominican Republic. Baseball.
WATT ** p

Alston, Walter Emmons. [also
known as Smokey]. 1911-1984.
United States. Baseball.
BABM ** p
BFAM * i
BGMA *** p
COAL *** p
MANG ** p, p/c
SGBM ** p

Alworth, Lance. 1940- . United
States. Football.
ASHT ** p
CHMP ** i/c
GPCP *** p
SPRN *** p

Ameche, Alan. 1933-1988.
United States. Football.
HATG **
HEIS ** p

Anderson, Donny. 1943- .
United States. Football.
SRBN *

Anderson, Ken. 1949- . United
States. Football.
DANF *** p
FWQB ** p
NFLS * p/c

Anderson, Sparky. [b. George
Lee]. 1934- . United States.
Baseball.
BABM ** p
MANG ** p, p/c
SGBM ** p

André the Giant. [b. Andrae
Rene Roussimoff]. 1946?-   .
France. Wrestling.
    WRES ** p

Andretti, Mario. 1940-   . Italy.
Automobile Racing.
    DOSW *** p
    DTDD ***
    GARD ** p
    GDGR *
    IRCD *** p, p/c
    KOMS *** p
    MARS *** p
    SMKR *** p
    WGRD *** p

Andrianov, Nikolai. 1952-   .
Union of Soviet Socialist
Republics. Gymnastics.
    WIGY ** p

Animal, The. [b. George
STEELE]. Birthdate? United
States. Wrestling.
    WRE2 ** p

Anson, Cap. [b. Adrian
Constantine]. 1851-1922. United
States. Baseball.
    BGMA ** p
    HOFB ** p
    HUNB ** p
    POBS ** p
    SGBM ** p

Aparicio, Luis Ernesto. 1934-   .
Venezuela. Baseball.
    BFAM * i
    GIML ** p
    TSBG ** p

Applebee, Constance. 1874?-
1981. Great Britain. Field
Hockey.
    HUNW ** p

Appling, Luke. [b. Lucius
Benjamin]. 1908?-   . United
States. Baseball.
    GAML **
    HOFB ** p
    HUNB ** p

Apps, Syl. [b. Sylvanus Marshall
II]. 1915-   . Canada. Hockey.
    HSPH *** p
    KOTR ** p

Arcaro, Eddie. [b. George
Edward]. 1916-   . United
States. Horse Racing.
    GUAR ** p/c
    SPIM ** p

Archibald, Nate. 1948-   . United
States. Basketball.
    BPLM ** p

Arfons, Art. [b. Arthur Eugene].
1926-   . United States.
Automobile Racing.
    GARD **
    SUPC *** p

Arfons, Walt. [b. Walter].
1917?-   . United States.
Automobile Racing.
    SUPC ** p

Arizin, Paul. 1929-   . United
States. Basketball.
    GSTN ** p

Armstrong, Henry. [also known
as Melody Jackson]. [b. Henry
JACKSON]. 1912- . United
States. Boxing.
    POBS ** p
    SHWQ *** p

Arnold, Billy. 1910?-1976.
United States. Automobile
Racing.
    GMIN ** p

Ascari, Alberto. 1918-1955.
Italy. Automobile Racing.
    WCHP *** p

Ashe, Arthur Robert. 1943- .
United States. Tennis.
    ASHT ** p
    CTTC ** p
    FATP *** p
    TENN **
    TDTL ** p
    WMOT ** p
    WNTC ** p

Ashford, Emmett Littleton.
1914-1980. United States.
Baseball [umpire].
    BWPL * p
    TDTL *** p

Ashford, Evelyn. 1957- . United
States. Track and Field.
    SWTR *** p
    TRGW *** p

Atlas, Tony. Birthdate? United
States. Wrestling.
    WRES ** p

Attles, Alvin. 1936- . United
States. Basketball.
    CCHA ** p/c

Auerbach, Red. [b. Arnold].
1917- . United States.
Basketball.
    THCF * p

Austin, Jimmy [also known as
Pepper]. [b. James Philip]. 1879-
1965. Great Britain. Baseball.
    GOTT *** p

Austin, Tracy. 1962- . United
States. Tennis.
    LGPS ** p
    MMWS *** p
    RCHN ***
    WUND ** p
    WWOT ** p

Babashoff, Shirley. 1957- .
United States. Swimming.
    FMAW *** p
    WSWM ** p

Babilonia, Tai Reina. 1961?- .
United States. Ice Skating.
    STOI *** p

Backlund, Bob. Birthdate?
United States. Wrestling.
    WRES ** p

Bacon, Mary. 1950?- . United
States. Horse Racing.
    HUNW ** p

Baer, Max. 1909-1959. United
States. Boxing.
    SFST ** p

Baines, Harold D. 1959-   .
United States. Baseball.
    BASS * p/c

Baker, Bubba. [b. James Albert
London]. 1956-   . United States.
Football.
    FPPR ** p

Baker, Buck. [b. Elzie Wylie].
1919-   . United States.
Automobile Racing.
    ARYL * p
    GARD * p

Baker, Buddy. [b. Elzie Wylie,
Jr]. 1941-   . United States.
Automobile Racing.
    ARYL ** p

Baker, Frank [also known as
Home Run]. [b. John Franklin].
1886-1963. United States.
Baseball.
    HHCR **
    HUNB ** p

Baker, Terry Wayne. 1941-   .
United States. Football.
    HATG *** p
    HEIS ** p

Balas, Iolanda. 1936-   .
Rumania. Track and Field.
    TRGW ** p

Bando, Sal. [b. Salvatore
Leonard]. 1944-   . United
States. Baseball.
    CAPS *** p
    HHCR ** p
    OTWU ** p

Banks, Chip. [b. William]. 1959-
United States. Football.
    NFLS * p/c

Banks, Ernie [b. Ernest].
1931-   . United States.
Baseball.
    AHRK **
    BFAM * i
    HUNB ** p

Bannister, Roger Gilbert.
1929-   . Great Britain. Track
and Field.
    GISP ** i
    GRLS ** p
    TRMM ** p
    SPIM ** p

Barkley, Doug. [b. Norman
Douglas]. 1937-   . Canada.
Hockey.
    UFTM *** p

Barney, Lem. [b. Lemuel
Joseph]. 1945-   . United States.
Football.
    CHMP ** i/c
    PFHT ** p

Barron, Ben. Birthdate? United
States. Track and Field.
    MARA ** p

Barron, Gayle. 1945-   . United
States. Track and Field.
    MARA ** p

Barry, Rick [b. Richard Francis
III]. 1944-   . United States.
Basketball.
    BBGM ** p

7

CHCH **
CHMP ** p/c, i/c
FORW ** p/c
HSPB *** p
PBGR **
WATT ** p

Bartz, Jennifer. 1955- . United
States. Swimming.
    WOWW ** p

Bass, Dick. [b. Richard Lee].
1937- . United States. Football.
    GRBF ** p
    GRUN ** p
    SRBN *** p

Bathgate, Andy. [b. Andrew
James]. 1932- . Canada.
Hockey.
    HGST **

Battles, Clifford Franklin. 1910-
1981. United States. Football.
    GRUN ** p
    HUNF ** p

Baugh, Laura Zonetta. 1955- .
United States. Golf.
    HUNW ** p

Baugh, Sammy. [b. Samuel
Adrian]. 1914- . United States.
Football.
    FCQB ** p
    GISP ** i
    GPQU ** p
    HUNF ** p
    SPIM ** p
    STOF * p

Baughan, Maxie. 1938- .
United States. Football.
    QLBN ** p

Baumhower, Bob. 1955- .
United States. Football.
    NFLS * p/c

Bayi, Filbert. 1953?- .
Tanzania. Track and Field.
    TRMM ** p

Baylor, Ed. [b. Elgin Gay].
1934- . United States.
Basketball.
    BBGM ** p
    FPBS ** p
    GSTN *** p

Beamon, Bob. 1946- . United
States. Track and Field.
    AMOS **

Beard, Frank. 1939- . United
States. Golf.
    BEYD **

Bearden, Gene. [b. Henry
Eugene]. 1920- . United States.
Baseball.
    SHWQ ** p

Beauchamp, Bobby. 1963?- .
United States. Ice Skating.
    STOI ** p

Beban, Gary Joseph. 1946- .
United States. Football.
    HATG **
    HEIS ** p

Beck, Gary. 1940?-   . United
States. Automobile Racing.
    MDRS *** p

Beck, Trudy. 1960?-   . United
States. Motorcycle Racing.
    WISM * p

Beckenbauer, Franz. 1946?-   .
West Germany. Soccer.
    HROS *** p

Becker, Boris. 1967-   . West
Germany. Tennis.
    YANF ** p

Beckert, Glenn Alfred. 1940-   .
United States. Baseball.
    GIML ** p

Bednarik, Chuck. [b. Charles].
1925-   . United States. Football.
    HUNF ** p

Belinsky, Bo. [b. Robert].
1936-   . United States.Baseball.
    CHCH *

Beliveau, Jean Marc. 1931-   .
Canada. Hockey.
    FHPL *** p
    HGAS *** p
    HGST **
    HOPH *** p
    HTSC ** p
    STOH ** p

Bell, Buddy. [b. David Gus].
1951-   . United States.
Baseball.
    OTWU ** p

Bellamy, Walt. 1939-   . United
States. Basketball.
    LONH ** p

Bellino, Joe. [b. Joseph Michael].
1938-   . United States. Football.
    HATG **
    HEIS ** p

Belmont, Joe. Birthdate? United
States. Basketball.
    COAL ** p

Belote, Melissa Louise. 1956-   .
United States. Swimming.
    CWSP *** p
    WISP ** p

Bench, Johnny Lee. 1947-   .
United States. Baseball.
    BATA ** p
    BEYD **
    BIBA **
    CACH ** p, p/c
    CHMP ** p/c, i/c
    GBST ** p
    MASK ** p
    MOBS ** p
    SOML *** p
    TSBG ** p

Bender, Charles Albert. 1883-
1954. United States. Baseball.
    GIND *** p
    HUNB * p

Benirschke, Rolf Joachim.
1955-   . United States. Football.
    FSTK ** p

Benoit, Joan. [m. Samuelson].
1957-   . United States. Track
and Field.
    TRGW *** p

Berenson, Red. [b. Gordon
Arthur]. 1939-   . Canada.
Hockey.
    HOPH *** p

Berg, Moe. [b. Morris]. 1902-
1972. United States. Baseball.
    BEYD **

Berg, Patricia Jane. 1918-   .
United States. Golf.
    AWIS **
    HUNW ** p

Berg, Sharon. 1955-   . United
States. Swimming.
    WOWW ** p

Bergey, Bill L. 1945-   . United
States. Football.
    ANFL *** p
    MSLB ** p, p/c

Berlenbach, Paul. 1901-   .
United States. Boxing and
Wrestling.
    GLTR *** p

Berra, Yogi. [b. Lawrence Peter].
1925-   . United States.
Baseball.
    AHRK **
    BFAM * i
    GBST ** p
    GCML *** p
    GISP ** i
    HOFB ** p

HUNB ** p
MASK *** p
TSBG ** p

Berry, Ray. [b Raymond].
1933-   . United States. Football.
    GPCP *** p
    HUNF ** p
    SPRN *** p

Bertelli, Angelo. 1921-   . United
States. Football.
    HATG **
    HEIS ** p

Berwanger, Jay. [b. John Jacob].
1914?-   . United States.
Football.
    HATG *** p
    HEIS ** p

Bettenhausen, Gary. 1941?-   .
United States. Automobile
Racing.
    ARYL ** p

Bettenhausen, Merle. Birthdate?
United States. Automobile
Racing.
    ARYL ** p

Bettenhausen, Tony. [b. Melvin
Eugene]. 1916-1961. United
States. Automobile Racing.
    ARYL ** p
    GARD ** p
    GDGR *

Bettenhausen, Tony Lee.
Birthdate? United States.
Automobile Racing.
    ARYL * p

Bierman, Bernie. [b. Bernard William]. 1894-1977. United States. Football.
    COAL **

Big Daddy *see* Garlits, Don

Big John Studd. Birthdate? United States? Wrestling.
    WRES ** p

Big Train, The *see* Johnson, Barney

Bikila, Abebe. 1932?-1973. Ethiopia. Track and Field.
    MARA **
    SOTO **
    WCMA ** p

Biletnikoff, Fred. [b. Frederick]. 1943- . United States. Football.
    RECS ** p, p/c
    SBML ** p
    SPRN *** p

Bing, Dave. 1943- . United States. Basketball.
    GCIS ** p
    GUAR ** p/c

Bingaman, Lester. 1926- . United States. Football.
    FOIB ** p

Bingay, Roberta Gibb. 1942?- . United States. Track and Field.
    MARA **
    WWOS ** p

Binkley, Les. [b. Leslie John]. 1934- . Canada. Hockey.
    UFTM *** p

Bird, Larry. 1956- . United States. Basketball.
    BSHP ** p
    GRLS ** p

Birdsong, Otis. 1955- . United States. Basketball.
    BSHP ** p

Bird, The *see* Fidrych, Mark Steven

Bjorkland, Garry. 1951- . United States. Track and Field.
    MARA *** p

Bjurstedt, Molla. [m. Mallory]. 1892?-1959. Norway. Tennis.
    HUNW ** p

Blackburn, Howard. 1858-1932. United States. Sailing.
    SING ** p

Blackwell, Jerry. Birthdate? United States. Wrestling.
    WRE2 ** p

Blair, Matt. [b. Albert Matthew]. 1950- . United States. Football.
    FHHL ** p

Blair, Wren. 1925- . Canada. Hockey.
    COAL *** p

Blake, Toe. [b. Hector]. 1912- .
Canada. Hockey.
    COAL **
    HGST **
    STOH ** p

Blanchard, Doc. [b. Felix
Anthony]. 1924- . United
States. Football.
    GISP ** i
    HATG *** p
    HEIS ** p
    HUNF * p
    STOF ** p
    WHET *** p

Blanchard, Theresa Weld *see*
Weld, Tee

Blanda, George F. 1927- .
United States. Football.
    FSTK ** p
    GNFL *** p
    HUNF ** p

Blankers-Koen, Fanny. [b.
Francina]. 1918- . Netherlands.
Track and Field.
    GOLG ** p
    HUNW ** p
    TRGW ** p

Blazejowski, Carol. 1956- .
United States. Basketball.
    MMWS *** p

Bleier, Rocky. [b. Robert
Patrick]. 1946- . United States.
Football.
    GIFC ***
    WNQT ** p

Blood, Johnny. [b. John Victor
McNALLY]. 1903-1985. United
States. Football.
    HUNF ** p

Blount, Melvin. 1948- . United
States. Football.
    FDDB ** p

Blue, Vida Rochelle. 1949- .
United States. Baseball.
    BCHP *** p
    BFIP ** p
    CHMP ** i/c

Blumberg, Judy. 1957?- .
United States. Ice Skating.
    STOI * p

Blyleven, Bert. [b. Rik Aalbert].
1951- . Netherlands. Baseball.
    BASS * p/c

Blyth, Chay. 1940- . Great
Britain. Sailing.
    SING ** p

Body, The. [b. Jesse VENTURA].
1952?- . United States.
Wrestling.
    WRES ** p

Boggs, Wade Anthony. 1958- .
United States. Baseball.
    BASS * p/c

Bonds, Bobby Lee. 1946- .
United States. Baseball.
    SOML ** p

Borg, Bjorn. 1956-   . Sweden.
Tennis.
    FATP *** p
    WMOT ** p
    WNTC ** p

Borotra, Jean. 1898?-   . France.
Tennis.
    FATP * p

Bossy, Michael. 1957-   .
Canada. Hockey.
    HOSS ** p
    SCIH *** p

Bostock, Lyman Jr. 1950-   .
United States. Baseball.
    SUSS ** p

Boston Strong Boy see Sullivan,
John Lawrence

Boswell, Charley. 1916-   .
United States. Golf.
    GIFC ***

Bottomley, Jim. [b. James
Leroy]. 1900-1959. United
States. Baseball.
    BFAM * i

Boudrot, Denise. 1953?-   .
United States. Horse Racing.
    WSHR ** p

Bower, John William. 1924?-   .
Canada. Hockey.
    GGPH *** p
    MITN *** p

Boy, Boston Strong see Sullivan,
John Lawrence

Boy, Nature see Nature Boy

Boyd, Oil Can. [b. Dennis Ray].
1959-   . United States.
Baseball.
    BPTH *** p

Boyer, Clete. [b. Cletis LeRoy].
1937-   . United States.
Baseball.
    GIML ** p

Boyer, Ken. [b. Kenton Lloyd].
1931-   . United States.
Baseball.
    GIML ** p

Brabham, Jack. [b. John
Arthur]. 1926-   . Australia.
Automobile Racing.
    GDGR * p
    GMIN ** p
    SMKR *** p
    WCHP *** p

Braddock, James J. 1905-1974.
United States. Boxing.
    SFST ** p

Bradley, Bill. [b. William
Warren]. 1943-   . United States.
Basketball.
    AOGL *** p
    GCIS ** p

Bradley, Bill. 1947-   . United
States. Football.
    FSSS *** p
    PFHT ** p

Bradshaw, Terry Paxton.
1948-   . United States. Football.
ANFL *** p
DANF ** p
FSSS *** p
FWQB ** p
NFLS * p/c
PFHT ** p
PROQ ** p
SBWL *** p
STOF * p

Brambilla, Vittorio. 1937-   .
Italy. Automobile Racing.
RACE ** p

Brazile, Bob. [b. Robert
Lorenzo]. 1953-   . United
States. Football.
FHHL ** p
MSLB ** p, p/c

Breedlove, Craig. 1938-   .
United States. Automobile
Racing.
GARD ** p
KOMS *** p
MSRS *** p
SUPC *** p

Bresnahan, Duke. [b. Roger P.].
1880-1944. United States.
Baseball.
HUNB ** p

Bressler, Rube. [b. Raymond
Bloom]. 1894-1966. United
States. Baseball.
GOTT *** p

Brett, George Howard. 1953-   .
United States. Baseball.
BASS * p/c
BHOT ** p
OTWU ** p

Brickley, Charley. 1898-1949.
United States. Football.
HUNF ** p

Bridgeman, Junior. [b. Ulysses].
1953-   . United States.
Basketball.
SPSP ** p

Bridwell, Albert Henry. 1884-
1969. United States. Baseball.
GOTT *** p

Brinker, Maureen Connolly *see*
Connolly, Maureen

Brock, Lou. [b. Louis Clark].
1939-   . United States.
Baseball.
GBST ** p
HITT ** p, p/c
RBML ** p

Brockington, John. 1948-   .
United States. Football.
GRUN ** p
PFHT ** p
RUNB ** p, p/c

Broda, Turk. [b. Walter]. 1914-
1972. Canada. Hockey.
MITN ** p
STOH

Brodeur, Richard. 1952-   .
Canada. Hockey.
    HFGO ** p

Brodie, John. 1935?-   . United
States. Football.
    GPQU ** p

Brody, Bruiser. Birthdate?
United States. Wrestling.
    WRE2 ** p

Brorsen, Metha. 1963?-   .
United States. Rodeo.
    WISR ** p

Brown, Bill. [b. William D.].
1938-   . United States. Football.
    GRBF *** p

Brown, Bob. [b. Robert
Stanford]. 1941-   . United
States. Football.
    PFHT ** p

Brown, Fred. 1948-   . United
States. Football.
    BSHP ** p

Brown, Jim. [b. James
Nathaniel]. 1936-   . United
States. Football.
    ASHT ** p
    FRRB ** p
    GISP ** i
    GPRB ** p
    GRBF*** p
    GRLS ** p
    GRUN ** p
    HUNF ** p
    RBPS ** p
    SPIM ** p

STOF * p
TDTL *** p

Brown, Larry. [b. Lawrence].
1947-   . United States. Football.
    GPRB ** p
    GRUN ** p
    PFHT ** p
    SRBN ** p
    WNQT ** p

Brown, Mordecai Peter. 1876-
1948. United States. Baseball.
    BFAM * i
    HOFB ** p
    HUNB ** p

Brown, Panama Al. [b. Alphonse
T.]. 1902-1951. Panama. Boxing.
    POBS *

Brown, Paul. 1908-   . United
States. Football.
    FOCC ** p
    HUNF ** p
    SGFC *** p
    STOF ** p

Brown, Pete Earlie. 1935-   .
United States. Golf.
    TDTL *** p

Brown, Roger. 1942-   . United
States. Basketball.
    UHPB *** p

Brown, Roger. 1937-   . United
States. Football.
    FOIB ** p

15

Brown, Walter. 1905-1964.
United States. Basketball
[owner].
    THCF * p

Browning, Pete. [b. Louis
Rogers]. 1861-1905. United
States. Baseball.
    PIBB ** p

Brugnon, Jacques. 1895?-1978.
France. Tennis.
    FATP **

Brumel, Valeri. 1942- . Union
of Soviet Socialist Republics.
Track and Field.
    GISP ** i
    TGCH ** p

Bryan, Jimmy. [b. James
Ernest]. 1927-1960. United
States. Automobile Racing.
    GARD ** p

Bryant, Bear. [b. Paul William].
1913-1983. United States.
Football.
    SGFC ** p
    STOF ** p

Buckner, Quinn. 1954- . United
States. Basketball.
    BPLM ** p

Budge, Don. [b. John Donald].
1915- . United States. Tennis.
    CTTC ** p
    FATP *** p
    TENN **

Bundy, King Kong. Birthdate?
United States. Wrestling.
    WRE2 ** p

Bunning, Jim. [b. James Paul
David]. 1931- . United States.
Baseball.
    SPML *** p

Buoniconti, Nick. 1940- .
United States. Football.
    WATT ** p

Burdett, Lew. [b. Selva Lewis].
1926- . United States.
Baseball.
    BWPL * p
    WATT ** p

Burgess, Smoky. [b. Forrest
Harrill]. 1927- . United States.
Baseball.
    HUNB ** p

Burns, Tommy. [b. Noah
BRUSSO]. 1881-1955. Canada.
Boxing.
    SFST ** p

Burroughs, Jeff. [b. Jeffrey
Alan]. 1951- . United States.
Baseball.
    BMVP *** p

Bussey, Shelia. 1950?- . United
States. Rodeo.
    WISR ** p

16

Butkus, Dick. [b. Richard
Marvin]. 1942-   . United States.
Football.
    ASHT ** p
    CHMP ** p/c, i/c
    GLBN *** p
    HUNF ** p
    LINE ** p, p/c
    PFHT ** p
    SPIM ** p
    STOF * p

Button, Dick. [b. Richard
Totten]. 1929-   . United States.
Ice Skating.
    SOTO **
    WOTI ** p

Butz, Dave. 1950-   . United
States. Football.
    FOIB ** p

Buzonas, Gail Johnson *see*
Johnson, Gail

Caldwell, John. Birthdate?
Australia. Sailing.
    SING **

Camp, Walter Chauncey. 1859-
1925. United States. Football.
    HUNF ** p

Campanella, Roy. 1921-   .
United States. Baseball.
    BFAM * i
    BLPC *** p
    BOBG ** p
    BTPL *** p, i
    CBHA *** p
    GBST ** p
    GCML *** p

HOFB ** p
HUNB ** p
MASK *** p
SMAA ***

Campaneris, Bert. [b. Dagberto
Blanco]. 1942-   . Cuba.
Baseball.
    BWPL ** p
    INFD ** p, p/c
    TSBG ** p

Campbell, Donald Malcolm.
1921-1967. Great Britain.
Automobile Racing and Boat
Racing.
    SPKS *** p
    SUPC *** p

Campbell, Earl Christian.
1955-   . United States. Football.
    FBAB ** p
    HATG **
    NFLS * p/c
    WHET ** p

Campbell, Malcolm. 1885-1949.
Great Britain. Automobile
Racing.
    SUPC *** p

Campbell, Robin Theresa.
1958?-   . United States. Track
and Field.
    WSTF ** p

Canseco, José. 1964-   . Cuba.
Baseball.
    BHNS *** p

17

Cannon, Billy. 1937- . United
States. Football.
　HATG **
　HEIS ** p

Caracciola, Rudolf. 1901-1959.
West Germany. Automobile
Racing.
　CHSP ** i

Carew, Rod. [b. Rodney Cline].
1945- . Panama. Baseball.
　BHOT ** p
　GBST ** p
　GLSF *** p
　HITT ** p, p/c
　SMAA **
　TSBG ** p

Carlos, John. 1945?- . United
States. Track and Field.
　BEYD **

Carlton, Steve. [b. Steven
Norman]. 1944- . United
States. Baseball.
　BCHP *** p
　BIBA **
　RBML ** p
　TSBG ** p

Carmichael, Harold. [b. Lee
Harold]. 1949- . United States.
Football.
　FSHR ** p

Carnera, Primo. 1906-1967.
Italy. Boxing.
　HWCH * p
　SFST ** p

Carr, Fred. [b. Frederick].
Birthdate? United States.
Football.
　MSLB ** p, p/c

Carter, Don. 1930- . United
States. Bowling.
　WATT ** p

Carter, Duane. 1913?- . United
States. Automobile Racing.
　ARYL * p

Carter, Duane Jr. 1951?- .
United States. Automobile
Racing.
　ARYL ** p

Carter, Gary Edmund. 1954- .
United States. Baseball.
　BASS * p/c

Cartwright, Alexander J. 1820-
1892. United States. Baseball.
　HUNB ** i
　PIBB ** p

Cartwright, Bill. Birthdate?
United States. Basketball.
　LONH * p

Carvajal, Felix. 1873?- . Cuba.
Track and Field.
　WCMA **

Casals, Rosemary. 1948- .
United States. Tennis.
　QOTC ** p
　WTEN ** p

Casper, Billy. [b. William Earl].
1931- . United States. Golf.
    ASHT ** p
    Golf ***
    GTGO *** p

Casper, Dave. 1951- . United
States. Football.
    FTTE ** p

Cassady, Hopalong. [b. Howard].
1934- . United States. Football.
    HATG **
    HEIS ** p

Cauthen, Steve. 1960- . United
States. Horse Racing.
    WUND *** p

Cawley, Evonne Goolagong *see*
Goolagong, Evonne

Cedeno, Cesar. 1951- .
Dominican Republic. Baseball.
    SOML ** p

Cepeda, Perucho. 1906-1955.
Puerto Rico. Baseball.
    POBS * p

Cerdan, Marcel Jr. 1916-1949.
France. Boxing.
    BEYD **

Chadwick, Florence May.
1918- . United States.
Swimming.
    AWIS ** p
    HUNW ** p

Chaffee, Suzy. 1947- . United
States. Skiing.
    HUNW ** p
    WISS * p
    WOSS ** p

Chamberlain, Wilt. [also known
as Wilt the Stilt]. [b. Wilton
Norman]. 1936- . United
States. Basketball.
    ASHT ** p
    BBGM ** p
    BSTG **** p
    FPBS ** p
    GRLS *** p
    GSTN ** p
    LONH *** p
    MBBS *** p
    PBBM **** p
    RDPS ** p
    SPIM ** p
    WATT ** p

Chamberlin, Guy. 1894-1967.
United States. Football.
    HUNF * p

Chance, Frank Leroy. 1877-
1924. United States. Baseball.
    BGMA ** p
    HUNB * p
    SGBM ** p

Charboneau, Joe. [b. Joseph].
1956- . United States.
Baseball.
    BWPL ** p

Charles, Ezzard B. 1921-1975.
United States. Boxing.
    POBS ** p
    SFST ** p

Chase, Hal. [b. Harold Homer].
1883-1947. United States.
Baseball.
    PIBB ** p

Cheevers, Gerry. 1940-   .
Canada. Hockey.
    GGPH *** p
    MITN **
    PHHT ** p

Cheng, Chi. [m. Reel]. 1944-   .
Taiwan. Track and Field.
    HUNW ** p
    SPKS *** p
    SUSS ** p

Chester, Ray. [b. Raymond].
1948-   . United States. Football.
    FTTE ** p

Chi Cheng see Cheng, Chi

Chichester, Francis. 1901-1972.
Great Britain. Sailing.
    SING ** p
    THSA *** p

Chin, Tiffany. 1968?-   . United
States. Ice Skating.
    STOI ** p

Chinaglia, Giorgio. 1946?-   .
Italy. Soccer.
    HROS *** p

Chiron, Louis Alexander.
1899-   . Monaco. Automobile
Racing.
    GDGR **

Chocolate, Kid see Sardinias,
Eligio

Ciccarelli, Dino. 1960-   .
Canada. Hockey.
    HOSS ** p

Cierpinski, Waldemar. 1950-   .
East Germany. Track and Field.
    WCMA ** p

Clark, Dutch. [b. Earl Harry].
1906-   . United States. Football.
    HUNF * p

Clark, Dwight. 1957-   . United
States. Football.
    NFLS * p/c

Clark, Eugenie. 1922-   . United
States. Scuba Diving.
    WSSD ** p

Clark, Jim. [b. James.] 1936-
1968. Great Britain. Automobile
Racing.
    CHSP ** i
    GDGR ** p
    WCHP *** p
    WGRD ** p

Clarke, Bobby. [b. Robert Earle].
1949-   . Canada. Hockey.
    CAPS *** p
    GCEN ** p/c
    HSPH *** p
    HSSE **
    KOTR ** p
    MHSS *** p
    PHHT ** p
    SOSW *** p
    WNQT ** p

Clarke, Fred. [b. Frederick
Clifford]. 1872-1960. United
States. Baseball.
    BGMA ** p

Clay, Cassius Marcellus Jr. *see*
Ali, Muhammad

Clemens, Roger William.
1962-   . United States.
Baseball.
    BHNS *** p
    YANF *** p

Clemente, Roberto Walker. 1934-
1972. Puerto Rico. Baseball.
    ASHT ** p
    BFAM * i
    BEYD **
    BIBA ****
    BOBG ** p
    CHMP ** i/c
    GLSF *** p
    HOFB ** p
    HUNB ** p
    MOBS ** p
    TSBG ** p

Cobb, John. 1899-1952. Great
Britain. Automobile Racing.
    SUPC *** p

Cobb, Ty. [also known as The
Georgia Peach]. [b. Tyrus
Raymond]. 1886-1961. United
States. Baseball.
    BATA ** p
    BEYD **
    BFAM * i
    BIBA ***
    GAML **
    GBST ** p

GISP ** i
GRLS ** p
HOFB ** p
HOHR ** p
HUNB ** p
RBPS ** p
SMAA ****
SPIM ** p
TSBG ** p

Cochet, Henri. 1901-   . France.
Tennis.
    FATP ** p

Cochran, Barbara Ann. 1951-   .
United States. Skiing.
    WISP *** p
    WISS ** p
    WOSS ** p
    WOWW ** p

Cochran, Linda. 1954-   . United
States. Skiing.
    WOWW ** p

Cochran, Marilyn. 1950-   .
United States. Skiing.
    WOWW ** p

Cochran, Mickey. [b. Gordon].
1924-   . United States. Skiing.
    WOWW *

Cochrane, Mickey. [b. Gordon
Stanley]. 1903-1962. United
States. Baseball.
    BIBA **
    BLPC *** p
    BTPL *** p, i
    GAML **
    GBST ** p
    GCML *** p

HUNB ** p
MASK ** p
TSBG ** p

Coe, Sebastian. 1956- . Great
Britain. Track and Field.
  TGCH *** p
  TRMM ** p

Colavito, Rocky. [b. Rocco
Domenico]. 1933- . United
States. Baseball.
  AHRK **

Colbert, Nate. [b. Nathan].
1946- . United States.
Baseball.
  SOML *** p

Collett, Glenna. [m. Vare].
1903- . United States. Golf.
  AWIS **
  HUNW ** p

Collins, Doug. 1951- . United
States. Basketball.
  GUAR ** p,p/c

Collins, Eddie. [b. Edward
Trowbridge]. 1887-1951. United
States. Baseball.
  BATA ** p
  GAML **
  HUNB ** p

Collins, Gary. 1940- . United
States. Football.
  GPCP *** p

Collins, Jimmy. [b. James
Joseph]. 1873-1943. United
States. Baseball.
  HHCR *

Comaneci, Nadia. 1961- .
Rumania. Gymnastics.
  GOLG ** p
  GRLS ** p
  MLRG ** p
  MWSS *** p
  RCHN ***
  WIGY ** p
  WWOS ** p

Comiskey, Charles Albert. 1859-
1931. United States. Baseball.
  PIBB *** p

Concepcion, David Ismael.
1948- . Venezuela. Baseball.
  TSBG ** p

Conerly, Charley. 1922- .
United States. Football.
  GIFC ****
  GPQU ** p

Conner, Bart. 1958- . United
States. Gymnastics.
  MLRG ** p
  WIGY ** p

Connolly, Maureen. [also known
as Little Mo]. [m. Brinker]. 1934-
1969. United States. Tennis.
  AWIS ** p
  CTTC ** p
  FWTP *** p
  HUNW ** p
  QOTC ** p

Connolly, Olga Fikotova *see* Fikotova, Olga

Connors, Jimmy. [b. James Scott]. 1952-   . United States. Tennis.
 CHCH **
 FATP *** p
 TENN **
 WMOT ** p
 WNTC ** p

Cook, Greg. [b. Gregory Lynn]. 1946-   . United States. Football.
 PROQ ** p
 SQBN *** p

Cooksey, Marty. [b. Martha]. Birthdate? United States. Track and Field.
 MARA * p

Cooper, Earl. 1886-1965. United States. Automobile Racing.
 GARD * p

Corbett, Gentleman Jim. [b. James John]. 1866-1933. United States. Boxing.
 BHWC ** p
 HWCH *** p, i
 SFST ** p, i

Cornette, Jim. Birthdate? United States. Wrestling [manager].
 WRE2 ** p

Cosell, Howard Cohen. 1920-   . United States. Sports Announcing.
 CHCH **

Costello, Larry. 1932-   . United States. Basketball.
 WATT ** p

Cotton, Henry. [b. Thomas Henry]. 1907-1987. Great Britain. Golf.
 GTGO *** p

Cournoyer, Yvan Serge. 1943-   . Canada. Hockey.
 CAPS *** p
 GWNG ** p/c
 PHHT ** p

Court, Margaret Smith. 1942-   . Australia. Tennis.
 FWTP *** p
 QOTC *** p
 WTEN ** p
 WWOT ** p

Cousineau, Tom. 1957-   . United States. Football.
 FHHL ** p

Cousy, Bob. [b. Robert Joseph]. 1928-   . United States. Basketball.
 FPBS ** p
 GSTN *** p
 SHWQ ** p
 SPIM ** p
 THCF ** p
 WATT ** p

Coveleski, Stanley Anthony. [b. Stanislaus KOWALEWSKI]. 1890-1984. United States. Baseball.
 GOTT ** p

23

Cowens, David William. 1948- .
United States. Basketball.
    BEYD **
    BHFL ** p
    CENT ** p/c
    GCPB *** p
    LONH ** p
    MBBS *** p
    ROOK ** p
    THCF * p

Cox, Diane. 1958?- . United
States. Motorcycle Racing.
    WISM ** p

Cox, Fred. 1938- . United
States. Football.
    FSTK ** p

Crabtree, Helen. 1915- . United
States. Horse Training.
    WSHR ** p

Craig, Jim. 1957- . United
States. Hockey.
    SCIH *** p

Cramer, Scott. Birthdate?
United States. Ice Skating.
    STOI ** p

Crawford, Wahoo Sam. [b.
Samuel Earl]. 1880-1968.
United States. Baseball.
    GOTT *** p

Cromwell, Nolan Neil. 1955- .
United States. Football.
    FDDB ** p

Cronin, Joe. [b. Joseph Edward].
1906-1984. United States.
Baseball.
    BATA ** p
    BGMA ** p
    GAML ***
    HUNB ** p
    SMAA ***

Crow, John David. 1935- .
United States. Football.
    HATG **
    HEIS ** p

Crowhurst, Donald. 1932-1969.
Great Britain. Sailing.
    SING ** p

Crowley, Jim. 1902-1986.
United States. Football.
    HUNF * p

Crozier, Roger Allan. 1942- .
Canada. Hockey.
    MITN ** p

Crump, Diane. Birthdate?
United States. Horse Racing.
    AWIS *

Cruyff, Johan C. 1947- .
Netherlands. Soccer.
    HROS *** p

Csonka, Larry. [b. Lawrence
Richard]. 1946- . United
States. Football.
    BEYD **
    FBAB ** p
    GPRB ** p
    GRUN ** p
    PFHT ** p

RUNB ** p, p/c
SBWL ** p
SRBN ** p
STOF * p

Cuellar, Mike. [b. Miguel
Santana]. 1937-   . Cuba.
Baseball.
    UHML ** p

Cummings, Terry. 1961-   .
United States. Basketball.
    BAPP ** p

Cunningham, Billy. 1943-   .
United States. Basketball.
    SOPB *** p

Cunningham, Glenn. 1910-1988.
United States. Track and Field.
    CBHA *** p
    GLTR ** p
    SHWQ ** p
    TRMM ** p

Curry, John. 1949-   . Great
Britain. Ice Skating.
    STOI **
    WOTI ** p

Curtis, Ann. 1926-   . United
States. Swimming.
    AWIS *
    HUNW ** p

Curtis, Isaac. 1950-   . United
States. Football.
    ANFL *** p

Curtis, Mike. 1943-   . United
States. Football.
    GLBN ** p

PFHT ** p

Cushman, Wayne. 1945-   .
Canada. Hockey.
    GWNG ** p/c

Cuthbert, Betty. 1938-   .
Australia. Track and Field.
    TRGW *** p

Daggett, Tim. 1963?-   . United
States. Gymnastics.
    MLRG ** p

Daniels, Mel. 1945-   . United
States. Basketball.
    UHPB *** p

Dantley, Adrian. 1956-   .
United States. Basketball.
    BAPP ** p

Darling, Ron. 1960-   . United
States. Baseball.
    BPTH *** p

Davis, Allen. 1929-   . United
States. Football.
    CHCH ***
    STOF *

Davis, Eric. 1962-   . United
States. Baseball.
    BHNS *** p

Davis, Ernie. 1939-1963. United
States. Football.
    HATG *** p
    HEIS ** p

Davis, Glenn. 1934-   . United
States. Track and Field.
  TGCH ** p

Davis, Johnny. 1955-   . United
States. Basketball.
  BPLM ** p

Davis, Junior. [b. Glenn].
1924-   . United States. Football.
  GISP ** i
  HATG *** p
  HEIS ** p
  HUNF * p
  STOF ** p
  WHET *** p

Davison, Ann. Birthdate? Great
Britain. Sailing.
  SING ** p
  THSA *** p

Dawkins, Pete. [b. Peter M].
1938-   . United States. Football.
  HATG *** p
  HEIS ** p

Dawson, Len. [b. Leonard Ray].
1935-   . United States. Football.
  FCQB ** p
  GPQU ** p
  PROQ ****
  SBWL ** p
  SQBN *** p

Day, Pea Ridge. [b. Clyde
Henry]. 1899-1934. United
States. Baseball.
  BWPL *

Dean, Daffy. [b. Paul D]. 1913-
1981. United States. Baseball.
  BWPL *
  BZAN * p

Dean, Dizzy. [b. J. Hanna].
1911-1974. United States.
Baseball.
  BFAM * i
  BIBA ***
  BOBG ** p
  BWPL ** i
  BZAN *** p
  HUNB ** p
  PIBB *** p

Dean, Fred. 1952-   . United
States. Football.
  FPPR ** p

DeBusschere, Dave. 1940-   .
United States. Basketball.
  UHPL *** p
  WATT ** p

Decker, Mary. [m. Slaney].
1958-   . United States. Track
and Field.
  HUNW * p
  SWTR *** p
  TRMM ** p
  WISP ** p

Delahanty, Ed. [b. Edward
James]. 1867-1903. United
States. Baseball.
  BFAM * i
  HUNB ** p

de la Hunty, Shirley Strickland
see Strickland, Shirley

DeLamielleure, Joe. 1951- .
United States. Football.
  FCBL ** p

DeLeeuw, Dianne. 1956- .
Netherlands. Ice Skating.
  STOI ** p
  WSFS ** p

Delvecchio, Fats. [b. Alex].
1931- . Canada. Hockey.
  WATT ** p

DeMar, Clarence H. 1888?-1958.
United States. Track and Field.
  MARA **

Dempsey, Jack. [b. William
Harrison]. 1895-1983. United
States. Boxing.
  BEYD **
  BHCF ** p
  BHWC ** p
  HWCH *** p
  SFST ** p
  SPIM ** p

Dempsey, Tom. [b. Thomas
John]. 1947?- . United States.
Football.
  BEYD **
  FSTK ** p
  WNQT ** p

Depailler, Patrick. 1944- .
France. Automobile Racing.
  RACE ** p

DePalma, Ralph. 1883-1956.
Italy. Automobile Racing.
  GARD ** p
  GMIN ** p

Devaney, Bob. [b. Robert S].
1915- . United States. Football.
  SGFC ** p

De Varona, Donna. 1947- .
United States. Swimming.
  AOGL *** p
  GOLG ** p

DiBiase, Ted *see* Million Dollar
Man

Dickerson, Eric. 1960- . United
States. Football.
  RBPS ** p

Dickey, Bill. [b. William
Malcolm]. 1907- . United
States. Baseball.
  BATA ** p
  BLPC *** p
  BTPL *** p, i
  GAML ***
  GBST ** p
  GCML *** p
  HUNB ** p
  SMAA ***

Didrikson, Babe. [b. Mildred
Ella]. [m. Zaharias]. 1911?-1956.
United States. Golf and Track
and Field.
  AWIS ** p
  CHOS *** p
  CWSP *** p
  DRID ** p
  GLTR *** p

GOLG *** p
GRLS ** p
HUNW ** p
SOTO ** p
SPIM ** p
TRGW ** p
WISP *** p
WWOS ** p

Dierdorf, Dan. [b. Daniel Lee].
1949-   . United States. Football.
FCBL ** p

Dillard, Harrison. 1923-   .
United States. Track and
Field.
GCIS ** p
TGCH ** p

DiMaggio, Joe. [also known as
Joltin' Joe and Yankee Clipper].
[b. Joseph Paul]. 1914-   .
United States. Baseball.
AHRK **
BEYD **
BIBA ***
BOBG ** p
CHAB *** p, i
GAML ***
GCIS ** p
GISP ** i
HOFB ** p
HOHR *** p
HUNB ** p
SMAA ***
SPIM ** p
TSBG ** p

Dionne, Marcel. 1951-   .
Canada. Hockey.
HOSS ** p

HSPH *** p
HSSE **
KOTR ** p
LGPS ** p
SCIH *** p

Dixon, George. 1870-1908.
Canada. Boxing.
POBS ** p

Dixon, Hewritt. 1940-   . United
States. Football.
SRBN * p

Dr. J. *see* Erving, Julius

Dog, Junkyard *see* Junkyard Dog

Donohue, Mark. 1937-1975.
United States. Automobile
Racing.
ARCD ** p, p/c
DOSW ** p
SSAR ** p
WGRD ** p

Dorsett, Tony. [b. Anthony
Drew]. 1954-   . United States.
Football.
HATG **
FBAB ** p
NFLS * p/c
WHET ** p

Drabowsky, Moe. [b. Myron
Walter]. 1935-   . Poland.
Baseball.
BWPL *

28

Dragon. [b. Rick STEAMBOAT].
Birthdate? United States.
Wrestling.
    WRES ** p

Drayton, Jerome. Birthdate?
Canada. Track and Field.
    MARA * p

Drechsler, Heike Daute. 1964-   .
East Germany. Track and Field.
    TRGW ** p

Dressen, Charles Walter. 1898-
1966. United States. Baseball.
    BGMA ** p

Dryden, Ken. [b. Kenneth
Wayne]. 1947-   . Canada.
Hockey.
    GFAW ***
    GGPH *** p
    GOAL ** p/c
    HSSE ***
    KOTR *** p
    MHSS *** p
    MITN ** p
    PHHT ** p

Drysdale, Don. [b. Donald Scott].
1936-   . United States.
Baseball.
    RBML ** p
    SPML *** p

Dudley, Bill. [b. William
McGarvey]. 1921-   . United
States. Football.
    GRUN ** p
    HUNF * p

Duncan, Jim. [b. James]. 1946-
1972. United States. Football.
    BEYD **

Durnan, Bill. [b. William
Ronald]. 1915-1972. Canada.
Hockey.
    GGPH *** p
    HGST **
    MITN ** p

Durocher, Leo Ernest. [also
known as Lippy]. 1905-   .
United States. Baseball.
    BGMA *** p
    COAL *
    SGBM ** p

Earle, Sylvia. 1935-   . United
States. Scuba Diving.
    WSSD *** p

Easley, Sonny. Birthdate?
United States? Automobile
Racing.
    DOSW * p

Ecker, Heidemarie Rosendahl
see Rosendahl, Heidemarie

Ederle, Trudy. [b. Gertrude
Caroline]. 1906-   . United
States. Swimming.
    AWIS ** p
    CWSP *
    GOLG ** p
    HUNW ** p
    SHWQ ** p

Ehmke, Howard John. 1894-
1959. United States. Baseball.
    BLPC *** p

Eller, Carl Lee. 1942-   . United
States. Football.
   DEFL ** p, p/c

Elliott, Herbert James. 1938-   .
Australia. Track and Field.
   TGCH ** p
   TRMM ** p

Ellison, Willie. [b. William
Henry]. 1945-   . United States.
Football.
   GRUN ** p

Elmer, Uncle *see* Uncle Elmer

Ender, Kornelia. 1958-   . East
Germany. Swimming.
   MOSS *** p

Erving, Julius. [also known as
Dr. J.]. 1950- . United States.
Basketball.
   BHFL ** p
   FORW ** p/c
   GRLS ** p
   HSPB *** p
   MBBS *** p
   PBGR **
   SOSW *** p

Esposito, Phil. [b. Philip
Anthony]. 1942-   . Canada.
Hockey.
   CHMP ** i/c
   FHPL *** p
   GCEN ** p/c
   HGST ** p
   HOPH *** p
   HTSC ** p
   MHSS *** p
   PHHT ** p

   SCIH *** p
   WATT ** p

Esposito, Tony. [b. Anthony
James]. 1943-   . Canada.
Hockey.
   GGPH *** p
   GOAL ** p/c
   HFGO ** p
   HSSE **
   MITN ** p
   PHHT ** p

Essegian, Chuck. [b. Charles
Abraham]. 1931-   . United
States. Baseball.
   WATT ** p

Evers, John Joseph. 1883-1947.
United States. Baseball.
   HUNB * p

Evert, Chris. [b. Christine
Marie]. [m. Lloyd]. 1954. United
States. Tennis.
   BEYD **
   FWTP *** p
   HUNW ** p
   MWSS *** p
   QOTC *** p
   SOSW *** p
   TENN **
   WWOT ** p
   WNTC ** p
   WTEN ** p

Eyston, George Edward.
1897-   . Great Britain.
Automobile Racing.
   SUPC **

Fabulous Moohlah, The *see* Moolah

Fairly, Ron. [b. Ronald Ray]. 1938- . United States. Baseball.
    UHML ** p

Fangio, Juan Manuel. 1911- . Argentina. Automobile Racing.
    CHSP ** i
    SMKR *** p
    WCHP ** p

Farina, Giuseppe. 1906-1966. Italy. Automobile Racing.
    WCHP *** p

Farr, Mel. 1943- . United States. Football.
    SRBN * p

Federspiel, Joe. Birthdate? United States. Football.
    MSLB *** p, p/c

Feller, Bob. [b. Robert William]. 1918- . United States. Baseball.
    BFAM * i
    BIBA **
    BLPC *** p
    GAML **
    HUNB ** p
    TSBG ** p

Fencik, Gary. 1954- . United States. Football.
    FDDB ** p

Ferguson, John Bowie. 1938- . Canada. Hockey.
    UFTM *** p

Fidrych, Mark Steven. [also known as The Bird]. 1954- . United States. Baseball.
    BWPL *** p

Figueroa, Ed. 1948- . Puerto Rico. Baseball.
    OTWU ** p

Fikotova, Olga. [m. Connolly]. 1933- . Czechoslovakia. Track and Field.
    AWIS ** p
    HUNW ** p

Fingers, Rollie. [b. Roland Glen]. 1946- . United States. Baseball.
    BARP ** p
    TSBG ** p

Finley, Chuck. [b. Charles O.]. 1918- . United States. Baseball [owner].
    CHCH ***

Fisk, Carlton Ernest. 1947- . United States. Baseball.
    BASS * p/c
    CACH ** p, p/c
    MASK ** p
    SOML *** p

Fitch, Bill. 1936?- . United States. Basketball.
    COAA ** p/c

Fittipaldi, Emerson. 1946- .
Brazil. Automobile Racing.
   IRCD *** p
   RACE ** p
   SMKR *** p
   SSAR ** p
   WCHP ** p

Fitzsimmons, Robert. 1862-
1917. Great Britain. Boxing.
   BHWC ** p
   HWCH ** p, i
   SFST ** p, i

Flair, Rick *see* Nature Boy

Flash, The Fordham *see* Frisch,
Frank Francis

Fleming, Peggy Gale. [m.
Jenkins]. 1948- . United
States. Ice Skating.
   AWIS ** p
   CWSP *** p
   GOLG ** p
   GRLS ** p
   HUNW ** p
   SOTO ** p
   WOTI ** p
   WSFS ** p

Fleming, Reggie. [b. Reginald
Stephen]. 1936- . Canada.
Hockey.
   UFTM *** p

Flock, Tim. [b. Julius Timothy].
1924- . United States.
Automobile Racing.
   GARD * p

Flood, Curt. [b. Curtis Charles].
1938- . United States.
Baseball.
   TDTL *** p

Flowers, Tiger. [b. Theodore].
1895-1927. United States.
Boxing.
   POBS *

Floyd, Raymond. 1942- .
United States. Golf.
   SSOG *** p

Flutie, Doug. [b. Douglas
Richard]. 1962- . United
States. Football.
   HATG *
   WHET ** p

Follmer, George. 1934- .
United States. Automobile
Racing.
   DOSW * p
   SSAR ** p

Ford, George. 1948- . United
States. Boxing.
   HWCH *** p
   SFST ** p

Fordham Flash, The *see* Frank
Francis Frisch

Ford, Phil. 1956- . United
States. Basketball.
   BPLM ** p

Ford, Whitey. [b. Edward
Charles]. 1928- . United States.
Baseball.
   BATA ** p

BFAM * i
BWPL ** p
GAML **
HOFB ** p
SMAA **

Foreman, Chuck. [b. Walter
Eugene]. 1950- . United States.
Football.
    FBAB ** p
    RUNB ** p, p/c

Fortmann, Danny. [b. Daniel
John.] 1916- . United States.
Football.
    HUNF * p

Foster, George Arthur. 1948- .
United States. Baseball.
    BAPH ** p

Foster, Rube. [b. Andrew]. 1879-
1930. United States. Baseball.
    POBS ** p

Fouts, Dan. [b. Daniel Francis].
1951- . United States. Football.
    DANF *** p
    FWQB ** p
    NFLS * p/c

Fowler, Bud. [b. John W.
Jackson]. 1854?- . United
States. Baseball.
    POBS ** p

Fox, Nellie. [b. Jacob Nelson].
1927-1975. United States.
Baseball.
    TSBG ** p

Foxx, Jimmy. [b. James Emory].
1907-1967. United States.
Baseball.
    AHRK **
    BFAM * i
    BGSL *** p
    BHRH ** p
    HUNB ** p

Foyt, A. J. [b. Anthony Joseph
Jr]. 1935- . United States.
Automobile Racing,
    ARCD ** p, p/c
    ASHT ** p
    CIND *** p
    DOSW *** p
    DTDD ***
    GARD *** p
    GDGR ** p
    GMIN *** p
    HSCR *** p
    MARS *** p
    SMKR *** p
    SPIM ** p
    SSAR ** p
    WGRD ** p

Francis, Russell Ross. 1953- .
United States. Football.
    FTTE ** p

Frank, Clinton Edward. 1915- .
United States. Football.
    HATG **
    HEIS ** p

Franklin, Tony. [b. Anthony
Ray]. 1956- . United States.
Football.
    FSTK ** p

Fraser, Dawn. 1937- .
Australia. Swimming.
GOLG ** p

Fraser, Gretchen Kunigk.
1919- . United States. Skiing.
AWIS **
HUNW ** p
SOTO **

Fratianne, Linda Sue. 1962?- .
United States. Ice Skating.
STOI *** p

Frazier, Clyde. [b. Walt].
1945- . United States.
Basketball.
GUAR ** p/c
HSPB *** p
MBBS *** p
PBGR ***
SOPB *** p
WATT ** p

Frazier, Joe. [b. Joseph].
1944- . United States. Boxing.
BEYD **
HWCH *** p
POBS ** p
SFST ** p
SPIM ** p

Frederick, Jane. 1952- . United
States. Track and Field.
WSTF ** p

Free, World B. [b. Lloyd].
1963?- . United States.
Basketball.
BSHP ** p

Freehan, Bill. [b. William
Ashley]. 1941- . United States.
Baseball.
GCML *** p

Fregosi, Jim. [b. James Louis].
1942- . United States.
Baseball.
HHCR ** p

Friedman, Ben. [b. Benjamin].
1905-1982. United States.
Football.
HUNF ** p

Frisch, Frank Francis. [also
known as The Fordham Flash].
1898-1973. United States.
Baseball.
HUNB ** p
TSBG ** p

Fuchs, Becky. 1955?- . United
States. Rodeo.
WISR ** p

Fuchs, Ruth. 1946- . East
Germany. Track and Field.
TRGW ** p

Fulks, Joe. 1921- . United
States. Basketball.
GSTN ** p

Fuller, Genia. Birthdate? United
States. Skiing.
WISS * p

Fuller, Peggy. 1955?- . United
States. Motorcycle Racing.
WISM ** p

Fuqua, Frenchy. [b. John].
1946- . United States? Football.
   BEYD **

Gable, Dan. 1949?- . United
States. Wrestling.
   BEYD **
   GIFC ***

Gabelich, Gary. [also known as
The Rocketman]. 1940- .
United States. Automobile
Racing.
   MSRS *** p
   SPKS *** p
   SUPC *** p

Gabriel, Roman. 1940- . United
States. Football.
   GPQU ** p
   PROQ *** p
   SQBN *** p

Gaedel, Ed. [b. Edward Carl].
1925-1961. United States.
Baseball.
   BWPL ** p
   BZAN ** p

Gagne, Greg. Birthdate? United
States. Wrestling.
   WRE2 **

Gallagher, Alan. 1945- . United
States. Baseball.
   HHCR **

Gans, Joe. [b. Joseph GANT].
1874-1910. United States.
Boxing.
   POBS ** p

Gardner, Randy. 1959?- .
United States. Ice Skating.
   STOI *** p

Garlits, Don. [also known as Big
Daddy]. [b. Donald Glenn].
1932- . United States.
Automobile Racing.
   GARD ** p
   MDRS ** p
   SPKS *** p
   SSAR ** p
   SUPD *** p
   WGRD ** p

Garner, Kati. [b. Nancy].
1953- . United States. Scuba
Diving.
   WSSD ** p

Garrett, Mike. [b. Michael
Lockett]. 1944- . United States.
Football.
   GRBF ** p
   GRUN ** p
   HATG **
   HEIS ** p
   SRBN ** p

Garvey, Steve. [b. Steven
Patrick]. 1948- . United States.
Baseball.
   BHOT ** p
   BMVP *** p
   INFD ** p, p/c

Garvin, Jim. Birthdate? United
States. Wrestling.
   WRE2 ** p

Gaylord, Mitch. 1961?- . United
States. Gymnastics.
    MLRG ** p

Gehrig, Lou. [b. Henry Louis].
1903-1941. United States.
Baseball.
    AHRK ***
    BATA ** p
    BFAM * i
    BHRH ** p
    BIBA ***
    BOBG ** p
    GAML ***
    GISP ** i
    HOFB ** p
    HOHR **** p
    HUNB ** p
    SMAA ****
    TSBG ** p

Gehringer, Charles Leonard.
1903- . United States.
Baseball.
    GAML **

Geiberger, Allen. 1937- .
United States. Golf.
    SSOG *** p

Genesko, Lynn. 1955- . United
States. Swimming.
    WOWW ** p

Geoffrion, Boom Boom. [b.
Bernard André]. 1931- .
Canada. Hockey.
    HGST **
    HTSC ** p

Georgia Peach, The see Cobb, Ty

Gerbault, Alain. 1893- .
France. Sailing.
    SING ** p
    THSA *** p

Gervin, George. [also known as
The Iceman]. 1952- . United
States. Basketball.
    BSHP ** p

Giacomin, Edward. 1939- .
Canada. Hockey.
    HOPH *** p
    MITN ** p

Giammona, Louie. 1953- .
United States. Football.
    SPSP ** p

Giant, André the see André the
Giant

Gibson, Althea. 1927- . United
States. Golf and Tennis.
    AWIS ** p
    BRIN *** p
    CHOS *** p
    CWSP *
    FWTP *** p
    GLTR *** p
    HUNW ** p
    QOTC * p
    TDTL *** p
    WWOS ** p
    WWOT ** p

Gibson, Bob. [b. Robert].
1935- . United States.
Baseball.
    ASHT ** p

BATA ** p
BFAM * i
CHMP ** p/c, i/c
GCIS ** p
RBML ** p
SPML *** p
TSBG ** p

Gibson, Joshua. 1911-1947.
United States. Baseball.
　　HUNB ** p
　　POBS ** p
　　SUSS ** p

Gibson, Moon. [b. George]. 1880-
1967. Canada. Baseball.
　　GOTT ** p

Gilbert, Gilles. 1949-　. Canada.
Hockey.
　　GOAL ** p/c

Gilbert, Rod. [b. Rodrique
Gabriel]. 1941-　. Canada.
Hockey.
　　PHHT ** p
　　WATT ** p

Gilchrist, Cookie. [b. Carlton C].
1935-　. United States. Football.
　　GRUN ** p

Gilliam, John Rally. 1945-　.
United States. Football.
　　RECS ** p, p/c

Gilmore, Artis. 1949-　. United
States. Basketball.
　　BHFL ** p
　　HSPB *** p
　　LONH **

Ginther, Richie. [b. Paul
Richard]. 1930-　. United
States. Automobile Racing.
　　GARD ** p
　　GDGR **

Gipp, George. 1897-1920.
United States. Football.
　　GISP ** i
　　HUNF ** p
　　STOF ** p

Glasgow, Nancy Payne see
Payne, Nancy

Glidden, Bob. Birthdate? United
States. Automobile Racing.
　　MDRS *** p

Gogolak, Pete. 1942-　.
Hungary. Football.
　　STOF * p

Golden, Maverick. [b. Bill].
1933-　. United States.
Automobile Racing.
　　KOMS ** p

Goldsworthy, Bill. [b. William
Alfred]. 1944-　. Canada.
Hockey.
　　HSSE **
　　PHHT ** p

Gomez, Lefty. [b. Vernon Louis].
1909-1989. United States.
Baseball.
　　BZAN ** p

37

Gonzales, Pancho. [b. Richard Alonzo]. 1928- . United States. Tennis.
BEYD **
CTTC ** p
FATP *** p
SPIM ** p
TENN **
WATT ** p
WMOT ** p

Gooden, Dwight. 1964- . United States. Baseball.
BASS * p/c

Goolagong, Evonne. [m. Cawley]. 1951- . Australia. Tennis.
FWTP *** p
HUNW ** p
QOTC ** p
TENN **
WNTC ** p
WTEN ** p
WWOT ** p

Gordon, Al. ?-1936. United States. Automobile Racing.
DTDD **

Goslin, Goose. [b. Leon Allen]. 1900-1971. United States. Baseball.
GOTT ** p

Gossage, Dick. [b. Richard Michael]. 1951- . United States. Baseball.
BARP ** p

Gould, Shane Elizabeth. 1956- . Australia. Swimming.
SPKS *** p

Grabarkewitz, Billy. [b. William]. 1946- . United States. Baseball.
HHCR ** p

Gradisher, Randy. 1952- . United States. Football.
FHHL ** p
MSLB ** p, p/c

Graham, Otto Everett Jr. 1921- . United States. Football.
FCQB ** p
GISP ** i
GPQU ** p
HUNF ** p
STOF * p
WATT ** p

Graham, Robin Lee. 1949- . United States. Sailing.
THSA *** p
SING *

Granatelli, Andy. 1923- . United States. Automobile Racing.
GDGR *
GMIN **

Grange, Red. [b. Harold Edward]. 1903- . United States. Football.
FBRN **** p
FRRB ** p
GISP ** i
GPRB ** p
GRLS ** p

GRUN ** p
HUNF ** p
POBS ** p
SPIM ** p
STOF ** p

Granger, Hoyle. Birthdate?
United States. Football.
    GRBF ** p

Grant, Bud. [b. Harold P].
1927-   . United States. Football.
    COAH ** p, p/c
    FOCC ** p

Grant, Frank Ulysses. 1867-
1937. United States. Baseball.
    POBS ** p

Gray, Leon. 1951-   . United
States. Football.
    FCBL ** p

Gray, Peter. [b. Peter J.
Wyshner]. 1917-   . United
States. Baseball.
    BEYD **
    GLTR *** p
    HUNB ** p
    SHWQ ** p

Graziano, Rocky. [b. Rocco
BARBELLA]. 1922-   . United
States. Boxing.
    WATT ** p

Green, Ted. [b. Edward Joseph].
1940-   . Canada. Hockey.
    BRIN *** p

Greenberg, Hank. [b. Henry
Benjamin]. 1911-1986. United
States. Baseball.
    BFAM * i
    GOTT **** p

Greene, Joe. [b. Charles
Edward]. 1946-   . United
States. Football.
    ANFL *** p

Greene, Nancy. 1943-   .
Canada. Skiing.
    WOSS *** p

Greer, Hal. 1936-   . United
States. Basketball.
    UHPB *** p

Gregg, Peter. 1940-   . United
States. Automobile Racing.
    RACE ** p

Gretsky, Wayne. 1961-   .
Canada. Hockey.
    GRLS ** p
    HOSS ** p
    RBPS ** p
    SCIH *** p
    WUND ** p

Grich, Bobby. [b. Robert
Anthony]. 1949-   . United
States. Baseball.
    OTWU ** p

Grier, Rosey. [b. Roosevelt].
1932-   . United States. Football.
    FOIB ** p

Griese, Bob. [b. Robert Allen].
1945-   . United States.
Football.
 CHMP ** p/c, i/c
 DANF *** p
 FWQB ** p
 PFHT ** p
 PROQ ** p
 QUAR ** p, p/c
 SQBN *** p

Griffin, Archie Mason. 1954-   .
United States. Football.
 HATG *** p
 WHET ** p

Griffith, Emile Alphonse.
1938-   . Virgin Islands. Boxing.
 WATT ** p

Groat, Dick. [b. Richard
Morrow]. 1930-   . United States.
Baseball.
 WATT ** p

Groh, Heinie. [b. Henry Knight].
1889-1968. United States.
Baseball.
 GOTT ** p

Grote, Jerry. [b. Gerald Wayne].
1942-   . United States.
Baseball.
 CACH ** p, p/c

Grove, Lefty. [b. Robert Moses].
1900-1975. United States.
Baseball.
 BATA ** p
 GAML ***
 HUNB ** p

TSBG ** p

Groza, Louis Roy. 1924-   .
United States. Football.
 FSTK ** p
 HUNF ** p
 STOF * p

Guerrero, Pedro. 1956-   .
Dominican Republic. Baseball.
 BASS * p/c

Guglielmo, Angelo. Birthdate?
United States? Baseball
[umpire].
 BWPL **

Guidry, Ron. [b. Ronald Ames].
1950-   . United States.
Baseball.
 BASS * p/c
 BFIP ** p

Gurney, Dan. [b. Daniel Saxon].
1931-   . United States.
Automobile Racing.
 GARD ** p
 GDGR *
 IRCD ** p

Gurney, Hilda. 1944?-   . United
States. Horseback Riding.
 WSHR ** p

Gushiken, Koji. 1957?-   . Japan.
Gymnastics.
 MLRG ** p

Guthrie, Bill. Birthdate? United
States. Baseball [umpire].
 BWPL **

Guthrie, Janet. 1938-   . United
States. Automobile Racing.
  DOSW ** p
  GMIN ** p
  MMWS *** p
  WWDA ** p, i

Gutierrez, Coco. [b. Cesar Dario].
1943-   . Venezuela. Baseball.
  RBML ** p

Guy, Ray. [b. William Ray].
1949-   . United States. Football.
  ANFL *** p

Guyon, Joseph Napoleon. 1892-
1971. United States. Football.
  HUNF ** p

Guzzwell, John. 1930-   . Great
Britain. Sailing.
  SING **
  THSA ***

Gwynn, Tony. [b. Anthony
Keith]. 1960-   . United States.
Baseball.
  BASS * p/c
  BHNS *** p

Hagen, Walter. 1892-1969.
United States. Golf.
  GOLF ***
  GTGO *** p

Halas, George. 1895-1983.
United States. Football.
  FOCC ** p
  HUNF ** p
  STOF * p

Hall, Glenn Henry. 1931-   .
Canada. Hockey.
  GGPH *** p
  HGST **
  HHOT *** p
  HMKM *** p, i
  MITN ** p

Hall, Jim. 1935-   . United
States. Automobile Racing.
  GARD **

Hall, Scott. Birthdate? United
States. Wrestling.
  WRE2 ** p

Ham, Jack Raphael. 1948-   .
United States. Football.
  FHHL ** p

Hamill, Dorothy. 1956-   .
United States. Ice Skating.
  GOLG **
  HUNW ** p
  MWSS *** p
  WOTI ** p
  WSFS ** p

Hamilton, Scott. 1958-   . United
States. Ice Skating.
  STOI ** p

Hammer, The. [b. Greg
VALENTINE]. Birthdate?
United States? Wrestling.
  WRES **

Hannah, John Allen. 1951-   .
United States. Football.
  FCBL ** p

Hansen, Stan. Birthdate? United
States. Wrestling.
  WRE2 ** p

Harmon, Tom. [b. Thomas D].
1919- . United States. Football.
  HATG *** p
  HEIS ** p

Harper, Terry. 1940- . Canada.
Hockey.
  PHHT ** p

Harper, Tommy. 1940- . United
States. Baseball.
  HHCR ** p

Harrelson, Bud. [b. Derrel
McKinley]. 1944- . United
States. Baseball.
  OTWU *** p

Harrelson, Ken. [b. Kenneth
Smith]. 1941- . United States.
Baseball.
  BWPL **
  WATT ** p

Harris, Bucky. [b. Stanley
Raymond]. 1896-1977. United
States. Baseball.
  BGMA ** p

Harris, Franco. 1950- . United
States. Football.
  FBAB ** p
  FSSS *** p
  SBWL ** p
  SOSW *** p
  STOF * p

Harroun, Ray. 1879-1968.
United States. Automobile
Racing.
  GARD *
  GMIN ** p

Hart, Eddie. 1948- . United
States. Track and Field.
  SUSS ** p

Hart, Leon Joseph. 1928- .
United States. Football.
  HATG *** p
  HEIS ** p

Hart, Marvin. 1876-1931.
United States. Boxing.
  SFST ** p

Hartack, Bill. [b. William John].
1932- . United States. Horse
Racing.
  WATT ** p

Hartnett, Gabby. [b. Charles
Leo]. 1900-1972. United States.
Baseball.
  GBST ** p
  GCML *** p
  MASK ** p

Harvey, Doug. [b. Douglas]. 1924-
1989. Canada. Hockey.
  HGAS ** p
  HGST **

Havlicek, John. 1940- . United
States. Basketball.
  CAPS *** p
  FORW ** p/c
  GCIS ** p
  GSTN ** p

MBBS *** p
PBGR ***
SOPB *** p
WATT ** p

Hawkins, Connie. 1942- .
United States. Basketball.
SOPB *** p
SUSS ** p
WATT ** p

Hawley, Don. ?-1974. United
States. Automobile Racing and
Motorcycle Racing.
DTDD ***

Hawthorn, John Michael. 1929-
1959. Great Britain. Automobile
Racing.
WCHP *** p

Hayes, Bob. [b. Robert Lee].
1942- . United States. Football
and Track and Field.
AMOS **
ASHT ** p
GISP ** i
GPCP *** p
SPKS *** p
SPRN *** p

Hayes, Elvin. 1945- . United
States. Basketball.
BHFL ** p
GSTN ** p
LONH *** p
SOPB *** p

Hayes, Johnny. 1886?-1965.
United States. Track and Field.
MARA **
WCMA **

Hayes, Lester. 1955- . United
States. Football.
FDDB ** p

Hayes, Woody. [b. Wayne
Woodrow]. 1913-1987. United
States. Football.
CHCH **

Haymond, Alvin Henry. 1942- .
United States. Football.
SRBN *** p

Haynes, Abner. 1937- . United
States. Football.
GRUN ** p

Haynes, Mike. [b. Michael
James]. 1953- . United States.
Football.
FDDB ** p

Haywood, Spencer. 1949- .
United States. Basketball.
BRIN *** p
HSPB *** p
SOPB *** p

Heath, Allen. Birthdate?
Canada. Automobile Racing.
GARD ** p

Hebner, Richard Joseph.
1947- . United States.
Baseball.
HHCR ** p

Heddy, Kathy. 1959?- . United
States. Swimming.
WSWM ** p

Heffelfinger, Pudge. [b. William Walter]. 1867-1954. United States. Football.
  HUNF ** p

Heiden, Beth. 1959- . United States. Ice Skating.
  WUND ** p

Heiden, Eric. 1958- . United States. Bicycle Racing and Ice Skating.
  WOTI ** p
  WUND *** p

Hein, Melvin John. 1909- . United States. Football.
  GLBN *** p
  HUNF ** p

Heinsohn, Tom. [b. Thomas William]. 1934- . United States. Basketball.
  THCF ** p

Heisman, John William. 1869-1936. United States. Football.
  HUNF ** p
  SGFC ** p
  WHET ** p

Heiss, Carol. [m. Jenkins]. 1940- . United States. Ice Skating.
  AWIS ** p
  GLTR ** p
  GOLG ** p
  HUNW ** p
  WATT ** p
  WSFS *

Henderson, Paul Garnet. 1943- . Canada. Hockey.
  PHHT ** p

Henderson, Rickey. 1958- . United States. Baseball.
  BASS * p/c

Hendricks, Ted. [b. Theodore Paul]. 1947- . United States. Football.
  FHHL ** p

Henie, Sonja. 1912-1969. Norway. Ice Skating.
  CWSP *
  GOLG *** p
  HUNW ** p
  SOTO **
  SPIM ** p
  WSFS *
  WWOS ** p

Henning, Anne. 1956?- . United States. Ice Skating.
  WISP *** p

Henry, Pete. [b. Wilbur]. 1897-1952. United States. Football.
  HUNF ** p

Herman, Babe. [b. Floyd Caves]. 1903-1987. United States. Baseball.
  BWPL ** p
  BZAN *** p
  GOTT ** p

Hernandez, Keith. 1953- . United States. Baseball.
  BHOT ** p

Herr, Tom. [b. Thomas]. 1956-   .
United States. Baseball.
    BASS * p/c

Herrera, Efren. 1951-   . Mexico.
Football.
    FSTK ** p

Herzog, Whitey. [b. Dorrel
Norman]. 1931-   . United
States. Baseball.
    BGMA *** p
    SGBM ** p

Heston, Willie. [b. William
Martin]. 1878-1963. United
States. Football.
    HUNF * p

Heyison, Marc. 1962?-   . United
States. Baseball.
    BPTH *** p

Hill, Calvin. 1947-   . United
States. Football.
    GRUN ** p
    SPSP ** p
    SRBN ** p

Hill, Graham. 1929-1975. Great
Britain. Automobile Racing.
    CHSP ** i
    GDGR * p
    WCHP *** p

Hill, Philip Toll. 1927-   . United
States. Automobile Racing.
    CHSP ** i
    GARD ** p
    KOMS *** p
    SMKR *** p
    WCHP *** p

Hillbilly Jim. Birthdate? United
States. Wrestling.
    WRE2 ** p

Hiller, John Frederick. 1943-   .
Canada. Baseball.
    GCIS ** p
    WNQT ** p

Hinkey, Frank. 1871-1925.
United States. Football.
    HUNF ** p

Hinkle, Clarke. [b. William
Clarke]. 1912-1988. United
States. Football.
    HUNF * p

Hirsch, Crazylegs. [b. Elroy].
1923-   . United States. Football.
    GPCP *** p
    HUNF ** p

Hlavaty, Jana. 1941-   .
Czechoslovakia. Skiing.
    WISS ** p

Hoad, Lewis. 1934-   . Australia.
Tennis.
    CTTC **

Hodges, Gil. [b. Gilbert
Raymond.] 1924-1972. United
States. Baseball.
    AHRK **
    GIML *** p
    TSBG ** p

Hogan, Ben. [b. William
Benjamin]. 1912-   . United
States. Golf.
    CHOS *** p

GCIS ** p
GLTR *** p
GOLF ***
GTGO *** p
SHWQ ** p
SPIM ** p
WATT ** p

Hogan, Hulk. Birthdate? United
States. Wrestling.
    WRES ** p

Hogue, Maxine Joyce King *see*
King, Micki

Holbert, Al. 1946- . United
States. Automobile Racing.
    RACE ** p

Holman, Nathan. 1896- .
United States. Basketball.
    FPBS ** p

Holzman, Red. [b. William].
1920- . United States.
Basketball.
    CCHA ** p/c

Hooper, Harry Bartholomew.
1887-1974. United States.
Baseball.
    GOTT *** p

Horn, Ted. 1910-1948. United
States. Automobile Racing.
    GARD ** p

Hornsby, Rajah. [b. Rogers].
1896-1963. United States.
Baseball.
    BATA ** p
    BFAM * i

BIBA ***
CHAB *** p, i
GBST ** p
GISP ** i
HOFB ** p
HOHR *** p
HUNB ** p
SMAA ****
TSBG ** p

Hornung, Paul Vernon. 1935- .
United States. Football.
    ASHT ** p
    GPRB ** p
    GRBF *** p
    GRUN ** p
    HATG *** p
    HEIS ** p
    WHET ** p

Horvath, Les. [b. Leslie.]
1921- . United States. Football.
    HATG **
    HEIS ** p

Hotchkiss, Hazel. [m.
Wightman]. 1886-1974. United
States. Tennis.
    QOTC *
    HUNW ** p

Houston, Ken. [b. Kenneth Ray].
1944- . United States.
Football.
    ANFL *** p

Howard, Elston Gene. 1930-
1980. United States. Baseball.
    GCML *** p
    MASK *** p

Howard, Frank Oliver. 1936- .
United States. Baseball.
    AHRK **

Howe, Gordie. [b. Gordon.]
1928- . Canada. Hockey.
    CHMP ** p/c, i/c
    FHPL *** p
    GCIS ** p
    GFAW ***
    GLTR *** p
    GRLS ** p
    HGAS ** p
    HGST ** p
    HOPH *** p
    HTSC ** p
    SHWQ *** p
    SPIM ** p
    STOH ** p

Howe, Mark Steven. 1955- .
Canada. Hockey.
    HSPH *** p

Howley, Chuck. [b. Charles
Louis]. 1936- . United States.
Football.
    GLBN ** p
    SBWL ** p

Hoy, Bill. [b. William Ellsworth].
1862-1961. United
States. Baseball.
    HUNB * p

Hrabosky, Al. [b. Alan Thomas.]
1949- . United States.
Baseball.
    BWPL ** p

Huarte, John. 1944- . United
States. Football.
    HATG *** p
    HEIS ** p

Hubbard, Cal. [b. Robert Calvin].
1900-1977. United States.
Football.
    HUNF ** p

Hubbell, King Carl. [b. Carl
Owen]. 1903-1988. United
States. Baseball.
    BFAM * i
    BIBA ***
    BLPC *** p
    HUNB ** p
    WATT ** p

Hubbs, Kenneth Douglass. 1941-
1964. United States. Baseball.
    GIML ** p

Hudson, Lou. 1944- . United
States. Basketball.
    SOPB *** p

Huggins, Miller James. 1880-
1929. United States. Baseball.
    BGMA *** p
    SGBM ** p

Hull, Bobby. [b. Robert Marvin].
1939- . Canada. Hockey.
    ASHT ** p
    CHMP ** p/c, i/c
    FHPL *** p
    HGAS *** p
    HGST *** p
    HHOT *** p
    HOPH *** p
    HTSC ** p

PHHT ** p
SPIM ** p
WATT ** p

Hull, Dennis William. 1944- .
Canada. Hockey.
PHHT ** p
UFTM ** p

Hulme, Denis Clive. 1936- .
New Zealand. Automobile
Racing.
GDGR ** p
SMKR *** p
WCHP *** p

Hundhammer, Paul. Birthdate?
United States. Baseball.
BPTH *** p

Hunt, James Simon Wallis.
1947- . Great Britain.
Automobile Racing.
MARS *** p
RACE ** p
SMKR *** p

Hunt, Ron. [b. Ronald Kenneth].
1941- . United States.
Baseball.
RBML ** p

Hunter, Catfish. [b. James
Augustus]. 1946- . United
States. Baseball.
BPTH **** p
CHCH **
PTCH ** p, p/c
SOML *** p

Huntley, Joni. Birthdate? United
States. Track and Field.
WSTF ** p

Hurtubise, Hercules. [b. Jim].
1931- . United States.
Automobile Racing.
GARD ** p
GLTR *** p
KOMS *** p

Hustle, Charley *see* Rose, Pete

Hutson, Don. [b. Donald
Montgomery]. 1913- . United
States. Football.
GISP ** i
GPCP *** p
HUNF ** p
STOF ** p

Iceman, The *see* Gervin, George

Imlach, Punch. [b. George].
1918- . Canada. Hockey.
COAL ** p

Insolo, Jimmy. Birthdate?
United States? Automobile
Racing.
DOSW * p

Iron Sheik, The. Birthdate?
United States Wrestling.
WRES ** p

Irvin, Monte. [b. Monford
Merrill]. 1919- . United States.
Baseball.
BFAM * i

Irwin, Hale. 1945- . United
States. Golf.
    SSOG *** p

Issel, Dan. 1948- . United
States. Basketball.
    UHPB ** p

Jack, Billy. Birthdate? United
States. Wrestling.
    WRES ** p

Jackson, Melody *see* Armstrong,
Henry

Jackson, Nell. 1929- . United
States. Track and Field.
    AOGL ** p

Jackson, Peter. 1861-1901.
Virgin Islands. Boxing.
    POBS ** p

Jackson, Reggie. [b. Reginald
Martinez]. 1946- . United
States. Baseball.
    BAPH ** p
    HITT ** p, p/c
    TSBG ** p

Jacobs, Helen Hull. 1908- .
United States. Tennis.
    FWTP *** p

Janowicz, Vic. [b. Victor Felix].
1930- . United States. Football.
    HATG **
    HEIS ** p

Jarier, Jean-Pierre. 1946- .
France. Automobile Racing.
    RACE ** p

Jarrett, Ned Miller. 1932- .
United States. Automobile
Racing.
    GARD ** p

Jefferson, John Larry. 1956- .
United States. Football.
    FSHR ** p
    NFLS * p/c

Jeffries, James Jackson. 1875-
1953. United States. Boxing.
    BHWC ** p
    HWCH ** p
    POBS * p
    SFST ** p

Jenkins, Carol Heiss *see* Heiss,
Carol

Jenkins, Ferguson Arthur.
1943- . Canada. Baseball.
    BCHP *** p
    BPTH *** p
    GFAW ***
    SOML *** p

Jenkins, Peggy Gayle Fleming
see Fleming, Peggy Gayle

Jenner, Bruce. 1949- . United
States. Track and Field.
    MOSS *** p

Jennings, Hugh Ambrose. 1869-
1928. United States. Baseball.
    BGMA ** p

49

Jim, Hillbilly *see* Hillbilly Jim

Joersz, Eldon. Birthdate? United States? Airplane Racing.
    MSRS *** p

Johansson, Ingemar. 1922- .
Sweden. Boxing.
    HWCH ** p
    SFST ** p

John, Tommy. [b. Thomas Edward]. 1943- . United States. Baseball.
    WNQT ** p

Johncock, Gordon. 1936- . United States. Automobile Racing.
    SSAR ** p

Johnson, Barney. [also known as The Big Train]. [b. Walter Perry]. 1887-1946. United States. Baseball.
    BATA ** p
    BFAM * i
    BLPC ** p
    GAML ***
    GBST ** p
    GISP ** i
    GRLS ** p
    HOFB ** p
    HUNB ** p
    RBPS ** p
    SMAA ***
    SPIM ** p

Johnson, Big Hands. [b. Gary]. 1952- . United States. Football.
    FPPR ** p

Johnson, Bob. [b. Robert D.]. 1946- . United States. Football.
    CAPS *** p

Johnson, Charley. 1938- . United States. Football.
    WATT ** p

Johnson, Dammy Williams. Birthdate? United States. Rodeo.
    WISR ** p

Johnson, Gail. [m. Buzonas]. Birthdate? United States. Swimming.
    WSWM ** p

Johnson, Gary *see* Johnson, Big Hands

Johnson, Gus. 1938- . United States. Basketball.
    UHPB *** p

Johnson, Jack. [b. John Arthur]. 1878-1946. United States. Boxing.
    BHCF ** p
    BHWC ** p
    HWCH ** p
    POBS *** p
    SFST ** p

Johnson, John Henry. 1929- . United States. Football.
    GRUN ** p

Johnson, Junior. [b. Robert Glenn]. 1931- . United States. Automobile Racing.
    GARD * p
    HSCR ** p

Johnson, Kathy. Birthdate?
United States. Gymnastics.
   MLRG * p

Johnson, Magic. [b. Earvin].
1959-   . United States.
Basketball.
   BPLM ** p

Johnson, Marques. 1956-   .
United States. Basketball.
   BHFL ** p

Johnson, Pete. [b. Willie James
HAMMOCK]. 1954-   . United
States. Football.
   FOIB ** p

Johnson, Rafer Lewis. 1934-   .
United States. Track and Field.
   SOTO **
   TDTL *** p
   TGCH *** p

Johnson, Ron. [b. Ronald
Adolphus]. 1947-   . United
States. Football.
   FSSS *** p
   GRUN ** p
   PFHT ** p
   SRBN *** p

Johnson, Trudy. 1965?-   .
United States. Rodeo.
   WISR * p

Johnson, Walter Perry *see*
Johnson, Barney

Johnston, Eddie. [b. Edward
Joseph]. 1935-   . Canada.
Hockey.
   WATT ** p

Johnstone, Jay. [b. John
William]. 1945-   . United
States. Baseball.
   BWPL ** p

Joltin' Joe *see* DiMaggio, Joe

Jones, Alan. 1946-   . United
States. Automobile Racing.
   SCHA *** p

Jones, Bert. [b. Bertram Hayes].
1951-   . United States. Football.
   FWQB ** p

Jones, Bobby. [b. Robert Tyre].
1902-1971. United States. Golf.
   GOLF ***
   GTGO *** p
   SPIM ** p

Jones, Bobby. 1951-   . United
States. Basketball.
   SPSP ** p

Jones, Deacon. [b. David].
1938-   . United States. Football.
   ASHT ** p

Jones, Kangaroo. [b. David
Jefferson]. 1880-1972. United
States. Baseball.
   GOTT *** p

Jones, K.C. 1932-   . United
States. Basketball.
   COAA ** p/c
   THCF ** p

Jones, Parnelli. [b. Rufus
Parnell]. 1933-   . United States.
Automobile Racing.
   ARCD ** p
   DOSW ** p
   DTDD ***
   GARD ** p
   GMIN * p
   WGRD ** p

Jones, Sam. 1933-   . United
States. Basketball.
   THCF ** p

Jones, Samuel Pond. 1892-1966.
United States. Baseball.
   GOTT ** p

Jones, Sue Sally. 1940?-   .
United States. Polo.
   WSHR ** p

Jordan, Lee Roy. 1941-   .
United States. Football.
   LINE ** p, p/c

Joyce, Joan. 1940-   . United
States. Golf. Softball.
   HUNW ** p
   MMWS *** p
   WWOS ** p

Juantorena, Alberto. 1952?-   .
Cuba. Track and Field.
   MOSS ** p
   TGCH ** p

Junkyard Dog [also known as J.
Y. D.]. Birthdate? United States?
Wrestling.
   WRES ** p

Jurgensen, Sonny. [b. Christian
Adolph]. 1934-   . United States.
Football.
   GPQU ** p
   PROQ *** p
   SQBN *** p

J. Y. D. *see* Junkyard Dog

Kabakoff, Harry. [b. Melville
HIMMELFARB]. 1927?-   .
United States. Boxing.
   COAL ** p

Kaline, Al. [b. Albert William].
1934-   . United States.
Baseball.
   AHRK **
   BEYD **
   RBML ** p
   WUND *** p

Kamm, Willie. [b. William
Edward]. 1900-1988. United
States. Baseball.
   GOTT ** p

Kapp, Joe. [b. Joseph]. 1938-   .
United States. Football.
   CHCH **
   SQBN *** p

Karsmakers, Pierre. 1946-   .
Netherlands. Motorcycle Racing.
   DTDD ***

Kazankina, Tatyana. 1951-   .
Union of Soviet Socialist
Republics. Track and Field.
    TRGW ** p

Kazmaier, Dick. [b. Richard W.].
1930-   . United States. Football.
    HATG *** p
    HEIS ** p

Keeler, Wee Willie. [b. William
Henry]. 1872-1923. United
States. Baseball.
    BFAM * i
    HUNB ** p

Keino, Kip. [b. Hezekiah
Kipchoge]. 1940-   . Kenya.
Track and Field.
    SOTO ** p
    TRMM ** p

Kell, George Clyde. 1922-   .
United States. Baseball.
    GAML ***

Kelley, John Adelbert. 1907-   .
United States. Track and Field.
    MARA **

Kelley, John J. 1930-   . United
States. Track and Field.
    MARA **

Kelley, Larry. [b. Lawrence
Morgan]. 1915-   . United States.
Football.
    HATG *** p
    HEIS ** p
    HUNF ** p

Kelly, King. [b. Michael Joseph].
1857-1894. United States.
Baseball.
    HUNB ** p
    PIBB *** p

Kelly, Leroy. 1942-   . United
States. Football.
    CHMP ** i/c
    GPRB ** p
    GRBF *** p
    GRUN ** p
    SRBN *** p

Kelly, Red. [b. Leonard Patrick].
1927-   . Canada. Hockey.
    FHPL *** p
    HGAS ** p

Kemp, Ray. [b. Raymond].
Birthdate? United States.
Football.
    POBS * p

Kemp, Steve. [b. Steven F.].
1954-   . United States.
Baseball.
    BPTH *** p

Kenyon, Mel. 1933-   . United
States. Automobile Racing.
    DTDD ***

Keon, Dave. [b. David Michael].
1940-   . Canada. Hockey.
    HOPH *** p
    PHHT ** p

Keough, Matt. 1955-   . United
States. Baseball.
    CSPS ** p

Kerr, John. 1932-   . United
States. Basketball.
COAL ** p

Kid Chocolate *see* Sardinias,
Eligio

Kid, The *see* Williams, Ted

Kiesling, Walter A. 1903-1962.
United States. Football.
HUNF * p

Kiick, Jim. [b. James F.].
1946-   . United States. Football.
GRUN ** p
SRBN *

Killebrew, Harmon Clayton.
1936-   . United States.
Baseball.
AHRK **
ASHT ** p
BHRH ** p
HHCR ** p
RBML ** p
TSBG ** p

Killy, Jean-Claude. 1943-   .
France. Skiing.
GRLS ** p
WOSS ** p

Kim, Nelli. 1957-   . Union of
Soviet Socialist Republics.
Gymnastics.
MOSS *** p
WIGY ** p

Kiner, Ralph McPherran.
1922-   . United States.
Baseball.
AHRK **
BHRH ** p

King, Bernie. [b. Bernard.]
1956-   . United States.
Basketball.
BSHP ** p

King, Billie Jean Moffitt.
1943-   . United States. Tennis.
AWIS ** p
CHCH **
CTTC ** p
CWSP *** p
FMAW *** p
FWTP *** p
GRLS ** p
HUNW ** p
QOTC *** p
TENN **
WISP *** p
WNTC ** p
WOWW *** p
WTEN ** p
WWOS ** p
WWOT ** p

King, Dolly. [b. William].
1916-   . United States.
Basketball.
POBS ** p

King, Micki. [b. Maxine Joyce].
[m. Hogue]. 1944-   . United
States. Swimming.
AOGL *** p
CWSP *
FMAW *** p
HUNW ** p

54

WISP *** p
WOWW *** p

Kingman, Dave. [b. David
Arthur]. 1948-   . United States.
Baseball.
    BAPH ** p
    HHCR *

Kinmont, Jill. 1938-   . United
States. Skiing.
    GOLG ** p

Kinnick, Nile Jr. 1919-1943.
United States. Football.
    HATG *** p
    HEIS ** p

Kirk, Tammy Jo. 1964-
United States. Motorcycle
Racing.
    WISM ** p

Kitt, Howard. 1942?-   . United
States. Baseball.
    BEYD **

Kittle, Ron. [b. Ronald Kale].
1958-   . United States.
Baseball.
    BPTH *** p

Klecko, Joe. [b. Joseph Edward].
1953-   . United States. Football.
    FPPR ** p

Klem, Bill. [b. William Joseph].
1874-1951. United States.
Baseball [umpire].
    BFAM * i
    HUNB ** p

Klosterman, Don. Birthdate?
United States. Football.
    GIFC ***

Knievel, Evel [b. Robert Craig].
1938-   . United States.
Motorcycle Racing.
    CHCH **

Knight, Pete. [b. William].
Birthdate? United States.
Airplane Racing.
    SPKS *** p

Koch, Bill. 1955?-   . United
States. Skiing.
    WOSS ** p

Koch, Marita. 1957-   . East
Germany. Track and Field.
    TRGW *** p

Kolehmainen, Hannes. 1889-
1966. Finland. Track and Field.
    MARA **

Koosman, Jerry. [b. Jerome
Martin]. 1942-   . United States.
Baseball.
    OTWU ** p

Korbut, Olga. 1955-   . Union of
Soviet Socialist Republics.
Gymnastics.
    GOLG ** p
    HUNW ** p
    MLRG ** p
    WIGY ** p

Koufax, Sandy. [b. Sanford BRAUN]. 1935- . United States. Baseball.
    ASHT ** p
    BATA ** p
    BFAM * i
    BOBG ** p
    GBST ** p
    GCIS ** p
    HOFB ** p
    HUNB ** p
    SMAA ***
    TSBG ** p
    WATT ** p

Kramer, Jack. [b. John Albert]. 1921- . United States. Tennis.
    CTTC ** p
    FATP *** p

Kramer, Jerry. [b. Gerald Louis]. 1936- . United States. Football.
    GLTR *** p
    HUNF ** p

Kramer, Ron. [b. Ronald John]. 1935- . United States. Football.
    FTTE ** p

Kunz, George. 1947- . United States. Football.
    CAPS *** p

Kusner, Kathy. 1940- . United States. Horse Racing.
    AWIS ** p
    CWSP *** p
    HUNW ** p
    MWSS *** p

Kwalick, Ted. [b. Thaddeus John]. 1947- . United States. Football.
    FSSS *** p

Lacoste, René. 1905- . France. Tennis.
    FATP ** p

Ladd, Ernest. 1938- . United States. Football.
    FOIB ** p

Ladewig, Marion. 1914?- . United States. Bowling.
    AWIS ** p
    HUNW ** p

Lady Maxine. Birthdate? United States. Wrestling.
    WRE2 ** p

Laffite, Jacques. 1943- . France. Automobile Racing.
    RACE ** p

Lafleur, Guy Damien. 1951- . Canada. Hockey.
    HOSS ** p
    HSPH *** p
    HSSE **
    KOTR ** p
    SCIH ** p

Lajoie, Larry. [b. Napoleon]. 1875-1959. United States. Baseball.
    HOFB ** p
    HOHR *** p
    HUNB ** p

Lambeau, Curley. [b. Earl
Louis]. 1898-1965. United
States. Football.
    HUNF * p

Lambert, Jack. [b. John Harold].
1952-   . United States. Football.
    FHHL ** p
    MSLB ** p, p/c
    NFLS * p/c

Lamonica, Daryle Pat. 1941-   .
United States. Football.
    SQBN *** p

LaMotta, Jake. [b. Jacob].
1921-   . United States. Boxing.
    BEYD **

Lancaster, Ron. 1938?-   .
Canada. Football.
    GFAW ***

Landry, Greg. [b. Gregory Paul].
1946-   . United States. Football.
    FSSS *** p
    PFHT ** p

Landry, Tom. [b. Thomas Wade].
1924-   . United States. Football.
    COAH ** p, p/c
    FOCC ** p
    SGFC ** p
    STOF * p

Lane, MacArthur. 1942-   .
United States. Football.
    SRBN ** p

Langer, Jim. [b. James John].
1948-   . United States. Football.
    FCBL ** p

Langford, Sam. 1883?-1956.
Canada. Boxing.
    POBS ** p
    SFST ** p

Lanier, Bob. 1948-   . United
States. Basketball.
    CAPS *** p
    GUAR *** p
    LONH ** p
    ROOK ** p

Lanier, Willie Edward. 1945-   .
United States. Football.
    GNFL *** p
    MSLB ** p, p/c

Largent, Steve M. 1954-   .
United States. Football.
    FSHR ** p
    NFLS * p/c

Larrieu, Francie. 1952-   .
United States. Track and Field.
    FMAW *** p
    HUNW ** p

Lattner, John Joseph. 1932-   .
United States. Football.
    HATG **
    HEIS ** p

Lauda, Niki. [b. Andreas
Nikilaus]. 1949-   . Austria.
Automobile Racing.
    CSPS ** p
    MARS ** p
    RACE ** p
    SMKR *** p

Laver, Rod. [b. Rodney George].
1938-   . Australia. Tennis.
    BEYD **
    FATP *** p
    SPIM ** p
    TENN **
    WMOT ** p

Lawrence, Andrea Mead *see*
Mead, Andy

Layden, Elmer F. 1903-1973.
United States. Football.
    HUNF * p

Layne, Bobby. [b. Robert
Lawrence]. 1926-1986. United
States. Football.
    GPQU ** p
    HUNF ** p

Layne, Floyd. Birthdate? United
States. Basketball.
    GIFC ***

Leach, Reggie. [b. Reginald
Joseph]. 1950-   . Canada.
Hockey.
    CSPS ** p

Leach, Tommy. [b. Thomas
William]. 1877-1969. United
States. Baseball.
    GOTT *** p

Leahy, Frank. 1908-1973.
United States. Football.
    COAL ** p
    HUNF * p
    STOF *

LeBaron, Edward W. 1930?-   .
United States. Football.
    HUNF ** p

LeClair, Jim. Birthdate? United
States. Football.
    MSLB ** p, p/c

Lee, Bill. [b. William Francis].
1946-   . United States.
Baseball.
    BWPL ** p

Lee, Sammy. [b. Soonkee].
1920-   . United States.
Swimming.
    GLTR *** p

LeFlore, Ron. [b. Ronald].
1952-   . United States.
Baseball.
    WNQT ** p

Lemm, Wally. 1919-   . United
States. Football.
    COAL **

Lemongello, Mark. 1955-   .
United States. Baseball.
    BWPL * p

Lenglen, Suzanne. 1899-1938.
France. Tennis.
    CTTC **
    FWTP *** p
    HUNW ** p
    QOTC *
    TENN **

Levegh, Pierre. 1905?-1955.
France. Automobile Racing.
    GDGR **

Lévesque, Jean-Louis. 1911-   .
Canada. Horse Racing.
    GFAW ***

Lewis, Carl. [b. Frederick
Carlton]. 1961-   . United States.
Track and Field.
    TGCH *** p

Lillard, Joe. [b. Joseph].
Birthdate? United States.
Football.
    POBS ** p

Lilly, Bob. [b. Robert Lewis].
1939-   . United States. Football.
    DEFL ** p, p/c
    PFHT ** p

Li Ning see Ning, Li

Link, Missing see Missing Link

Lindsay, Ted. [b. Robert Blake].
1925-   . Canada. Hockey.
    FHPL *** p
    HGAS ** p
    HGST **
    HTSC ** p

Lipscomb, Gene. [b. Eugene].
1931-   . United States. Football.
    FOIB ** p

Liston, Sonny. [b. Charles].
1932-1970. United States.
Boxing.
    HWCH *** p
    POBS ** p
    SFST ** p

Little, Floyd Douglas. 1942-   .
United States. Football.
    GPRB ** p
    GRUN ** p
    SRBN *** p

Little, Larry C. 1945-   . United
States. Football.
    ANFL *** p
    GNFL *** p

Little Mo see Connolly, Maureen
Catherine

Liut, Mike. 1956?-   . Canada.
Hockey.
    HFGO ** p

Lloyd, Christine Marie Evert see
Evert, Chris

Lloyd, John Henry. 1884-1965.
United States. Baseball.
    POBS ** p

Lobert, Hans. [b. John Bernard].
1881-1968. United States.
Baseball.
    GOTT *** p

Lockhart, Frank. 1903?-1928.
United States. Automobile
Racing.
    GARD * p

Lofton, James David. 1956-   .
United States. Football.
    NFLS * p/c

Lolich, Mickey. [b. Michael
Stephen]. 1940-   . United
States. Baseball.
    TSBG ** p

Lombardi, Ernie. 1908-1977.
United States. Baseball.
    GCML *** p

Lombardi, Lella. 1943-   . Italy.
Automobile Racing.
    RACE ** p

Lombardi, Vince. [b. Vincent
Thomas]. 1913-1970. United
States. Football.
    FOCC ** p
    HUNF ** p
    SGFC *** p
    STOF *** p

Longboat, Tom. 1887-1949.
Canada. Track and Field.
    MARA *

Loock, Christine. 1954?-   .
United States. Swimming.
    WSWM ** p

Lopez, Al. [b. Alfonso Ramon].
1908-   . United States.
Baseball.
    BGMA ** p

Lopez, Nancy. 1957-   . United
States. Golf.
    MMWS *** p

Lorenzen, Fred. 1934-   . United
States. Automobile Racing.
    GARD ** p
    HSCR ** p

KOMS **

Loscutoff, Jim. [b. James].
1930-   . United States.
Basketball.
    THCF ** p

Lott, Ronnie. [b. Ronald
Mandel]. 1959-   . United States.
Football.
    FDDB ** p

Loues, Spyridon. 1872-1940.
Greece. Track and Field.
    MARA **
    WCMA **

Louis, Joe. [b. Joe Louis
BARROW]. 1914-1981. United
States. Boxing.
    BEYD **
    BHCF ** p
    BHWC ** p
    GCIS ** p
    HWCH *** p
    POBS ** p
    SFST ** p
    SPIM ** p

Louis, Spyros see Loues,
Spiridon

Love, Bob. 1942-   . United
States. Basketball.
    UHPB *** p

Lovellette, Clyde. 1929-   .
United States. Basketball.
    WATT ** p

Lowenstein, John Lee. 1947- .
United States. Baseball.
    BWPL ** p

Lucas, Jerry. 1940- . United
States. Basketball.
    BBGM ** p
    FPBS ** p

Lucas, John. 1953- . United
States. Basketball.
    BPLM ** p

Lucas, Maurice. 1952- . United
States. Basketball.
    BAPP ** p

Luciano, Ron. [b. Ronald M.].
1937?- . United States?
Baseball [umpire].
    BWPL ** p

Luckman, Sidney. 1916- .
United States. Football.
    FCQB ** p
    GPQU ** p
    HUNF ** p
    STOF ** p

Lugar, Lex. [b. Lawrence].
Birthdate? United States.
Wrestling.
    WRE2 ** p

Lujack, John C. 1925- . United
States. Football.
    HATG **
    HEIS ** p

Lunger, Brett. 1945- . United
States. Automobile Racing.
    RACE ** p

Lurtsema, Bob. [b. Robert Ross].
1942- . United States.
Baseball.
    SPSP ** p

Lyle, Sparky. [b. Albert Walter].
1944- . United States.
Baseball.
    BARP ** p
    BWPL ** p

Lyman, Link. [b. William Roy].
1898-1972. United States.
Football.
    HUNF * p

Lynn, Fred. [b. Frederic
Michael]. 1952- . United
States. Baseball.
    BHOT ** p
    BMVP *** p

Lynn, Janet. [b. Janet Lynn
NOWICKI]. 1953- . United
States. Ice Skating.
    FMAW *** p
    HUNW ** p
    STOI ** p
    WOWW *** p
    WSFS ** p

McAdoo, Bob. [b. Robert].
1951- . United States.
Basketball.
    BHFL ** p
    CENT ** p/c
    GCPB *** p
    LONH * p
    PBGR ***

McAfee, George Anderson.
1918- . United States.
Football.
    GRUN ** p
    HUNF * p

McAlister, Jim. [b. James
Robert]. 1957- . United States.
Soccer.
    HROS *** p
    MSSS *** p

Macauley, Ed. 1928- . United
States. Basketball.
    THCF * p

McCarthy, Joe. [b. Joseph
Vincent]. 1887-1978. United
States. Baseball.
    BGMA *** p
    SGBM *** p

McCarver, Tim. [b. James
Timothy]. 1941- . United
States. Baseball.
    GCML *** p

McCluskey, Roger. 1930- .
United States. Automobile
Racing.
    DOSW * p
    SSAR ** p

McCormick, Patty. [b. Patricia
KELLER]. 1930- . United
States. Swimming.
    AWIS ** p
    HUNW ** p

McCovey, Stretch. [b. Willie
Lee]. 1938- . United States.
Baseball.
    AHRK **
    GIML ** p
    TSBG ** p

McCreary, Conn. 1921-1979.
United States. Horse Racing.
    SHWQ *** p

McCutcheon, Floretta. 1888-
1966. United States. Bowling.
    AWIS **
    HUNW ** p

McDaniels, Jim. 1948- . United
States. Basketball.
    LONH ** p

McDonald, Henry. 1890?-1976.
Haiti. Football.
    POBS ** p

McDonald, Tommy. [b. Thomas
Franklin]. 1934- . United
States. Football.
    GPCP *** p

McDowell, Sam. [b. Samuel
Edward]. 1942- . United
States. Baseball.
    RBML ** p
    SPML *** p

McElhenny, Hugh. 1928- .
United States. Football.
    FRRB ** p
    GPRB ** p
    GRBF ** p
    GRUN ** p
    STOF * p

McElreath, Jim. 1928-   . United
States. Automobile Racing.
    DOSW * p

McEnroe, John. 1959-   . United
States. Tennis.
    WMOT ** p
    WUND ** p

McEvoy, Michele. 1954?-   .
United States. Horse Racing.
    WSHR ** p

McEwen, Mongoose. [b. Tom].
Birthdate? United States.
Automobile Racing.
    GARD * p
    MDRS *** p

McGee, Willie. 1958-   . United
States. Baseball.
    BASS * p/c

McGill, Billy. 1939-   . United
States. Basketball.
    LONH ** p

McGinnis, George. 1950-   .
United States. Basketball.
    FORW ** p/c
    HSPB *** p

McGinnity, Joe. [b. Joseph
Jerome]. 1871?-1929. United
States. Baseball.
    BFAM * i
    HUNB ** p

McGraw, Muggsy. [b. John
Joseph]. 1873-1934. United
States. Baseball.
    BABM ** p

BFAM * i
BGMA *** p
HHCR *
HOFB ** p
HUNB ** p
SGBM *** p
TSBG ** p

McGraw, Tug. [b. Frank Edwin].
1944-   . United States.
Baseball.
    BARP ** p

McGregor, Rob Roy. [b. John].
1825-1892. Great Britain.
Sailing.
    SING ** i

Macho Man. [also known as
Randy Savage]. Birthdate?
United States.
Wrestling.
    WRE2 ** p

MacInnis, Nina. 1954-   . United
States. Swimming.
    WOWW ** p

Mack, Connie. [b. Cornelius
Alexander McGILLICUDDY].
1862-1956. United States.
Baseball.
    BABM ** p
    BFAM * i
    BGMA *** p
    HUNB ** p
    PIBB *** p
    SGBM *** p

McKay, John Harvey. 1923-   .
United States. Football.
    COAL ** p

McKechnie, Bill. [b. William
Boyd]. 1886-1965. United
States. Baseball.
    BGMA ** p

Mackey, John. 1941-   . United
States. Football.
    FTTE ** p
    GPCP *** p
    TDTL *** p

McKinney, Steve. 1953?-   .
United States. Skiing.
    WOSS ** p

McKoy, Wayne. Birthdate?
United States. Basketball.
    LONH **

McLain, Denny. [b. Dennis
Dale]. 1944-   . United States.
Baseball.
    ASHT ** p
    SPML *** p

McLaren, Bruce. 1937-1970.
New Zealand. Automobile
Racing.
    GDGR ** p
    WGRD *** p

McMahon, Vince Jr. 1945?-   .
United States. Wrestling
[promoter].
    WRE2 ** p

McMullen, Ken. [b. Kenneth
Lee]. 1942-   . United States.
Baseball.
    HHCR **

McNally, John Victor see Blood,
Johnny

McNamara, Julianne. 1966-   .
United States. Gymnastics.
    MLRG * p

Magerkurth, George Levi. 1888-
1966. United States. Baseball
[umpire].
    BWPL *

Magnum, T. A. [b. Terry Allen].
Birthdate? United States.
Wrestling.
    WRE2 ** p

Magnuson, Keith Arien. 1947-   .
Canada. Hockey.
    HSSE **

Magnussen, Karen. 1952-   .
Canada. Ice Skating.
    WSFS ** p

Mahovlich, Frank. [b. Francis
William]. 1938-   . Canada.
Hockey.
    HGST ** p
    HTSC ** p
    PHHT ** p

Mallory, Molla Bjurstedt *see* Bjurstedt, Molla

Malone, Moses. 1956-   . United States. Basketball.
   BAPP ** p
   BHFL ** p
   LONH ** p
   WUND *** p

Maloney, Jim. [b. James William]. 1940-   . United States. Baseball.
   SPML ** p

Man, Macho *see* Macho Man

Man, Million Dollar *see* Million Dollar Man

Man, Moon *see* Minton, Greg

Mann, Carol. 1941-   . United States. Golf.
   AWIS * p

Manning, Archie. [b. Elisha Archibald]. 1949-   . United States. Football.
   FSSS *** p
   FWQB ** p

Manning, Madeline. 1948-   . United States. Track and Field.
   SWTR *** p

Mantle, Mickey Charles. 1931-   . United States. Baseball.
   AHRK **
   BFAM * i
   BHRH ** p

BIBA ***
BOBG ** p
BRIN *** p
CHOS *** p
GAML ***
GCIS ** p
GISP ** i
HOFB ** p
HUNB ** p
RBML ** p
SHWQ *** p
TSBG ** p
WATT ** p

Maranville, Rabbit. [b. Walter James]. 1891-1954. United States. Baseball.
   BWPL * p
   BZAN *** p
   HOFB ** p
   HUNB ** p

Maravich, Peter Press. 1948-1988. United States. Basketball.
   ASHT ** p
   CHMP ** i/c
   GUAR ** p/c
   HSPB *** p
   PBGR **
   ROOK **** p

Marble, Alice. 1913-   . United States. Tennis.
   FWTP *** p
   QOTC * p

Marciano, Rocky. [b. Rocco MARCHEGIANO]. 1923-1969. United States. Boxing.
   BHWC ** p
   HWCH ** p
   SFST ** p

SPIM ** p

Marcol, Chester. 1948-   .
Poland. Football.
    FSSS *** p

Marichal, Juan Antonio.
1937-   . Dominican Republic.
Baseball.
    ASHT ** p
    SPML *** p

Maris, Roger Eugene. 1934-1985.
United States. Baseball.
    ASHT ** p
    BEYD **
    BHRH ** p
    GBST ** p

Marquard, Rube. [b. Richard
William]. 1889-1980. United
States. Baseball.
    BFAM * i
    BRIN *** p
    GOTT *** p
    HUNB ** p

Marshall, Jim. [b. James
Lawrence]. 1937-   . United
States. Football.
    DEFL ** p, p/c

Marshall, Mike. [b. Michael
Grant]. 1943-   . United States.
Baseball.
    BFIP ** p
    CHCH **
    PTCH ** p, p/c

Martel, Rick. Birthdate? Canada.
Wrestling.
    WRES ** p

Martin, Billy. [b. Alfred Manuel
PESANO]. 1928-1989. United
States. Baseball.
    BABM ** p
    BGMA *** p
    MANG ** p, p/c

Martin, Dugie. [b. Slater].
1925-   . United States.
Basketball.
    FPBS ** p

Martin, Harvey. 1950-   . United
States. Football.
    FPPR ** p
    SBWL ** p

Martin, LaRue. Birthdate?
United States. Basketball.
    LONH ** p

Martin, Pepper. [b. John
Leonard]. 1904-1965. United
States. Baseball.
    BZAN * p

Martin, Rick. [b. Richard Lionel].
1951-   . Canada. Hockey.
    GWNG ** p/c
    HSPH *** p
    HSSE **
    PHHT ** p

Mascaras, Mil. Birthdate?
Mexico. Wrestling.
    WRES ** p

Mason, Cathy Rigby *see* Rigby, Cathy

Mass, Jochen. 1946- . West Germany. Automobile Racing.
    RACE ** p

Mathews, Eddie. [b. Edwin Lee]. 1931- . United States. Baseball.
    AHRK **
    HHCR * p
    HUNB ** p
    TSBG ** p

Mathewson, Christy. [b. Christopher]. 1880-1925. United States. Baseball.
    DATA ** p
    BFAM * i
    BLPC ** p
    HOFB ** p
    HUNB ** p
    SMAA ****
    TSBG ** p

Mathias, Bob. [b. Robert Bruce]. 1930- . United States. Track and Field.
    AMOS **
    AOGL *** p
    GISP ** i
    GRLS ** p
    SOTO ** p
    TGCH ** p
    WUND *** p

Matlack, Johnny. [b. Jonathan T]. 1950- . United States. Baseball.
    OTWU ** p

Matson, Ollie. [b. Oliver Genoa]. 1930- . United States. Football.
    FRRB ** p

Matson, Randy. [b. Randel]. 1945- . United States. Track and Field.
    GISP ** i

Matthews, Vincent Edward. 1947- . United States. Track and Field
    AOGL *** p

Mattingly, Don. [b. Donald Arthur]. 1962- . United States. Baseball.
    BASS * p/c
    BHNS *** p

Mauermayer, Gisela. 1914?- . West Germany. Track and Field.
    BEYD **

Maxine, Lady *see* Lady Maxine

Mayberry, John Claiborne. 1950- . United States. Baseball.
    SOML ** p

Maynard, Don. [b. Donald Rogers]. 1937?- . United States. Football.
    GPCP *** p
    SPRN *** p

Mays, Carl William. 1891-1971. United States. Baseball.
    HUNB ** p

Mays, Rex. 1913-1949. United
States. Automobile Racing.
GARD * p

Mays, Willie Howard. [also
known as The Say Hey Kid].
1931- . United States.
Baseball.
AHRK ***
ASHT ** p
BATA ** p
BFAM * i
BGSL *** p
BHRH ** p
BIBA ***
BOBG ** p
CHCH **
CHMP ** p/c, i/c
GISP ** i
GRLS ** p
HUNB ** p
MOBS ** p
RBML ** p
SMAA ***
SPIM ** p
TSBG ** p
WATT ** p

Mead, Andy. [b. Andrea]. [m.
Lawrence]. 1932- . United
States. Skiing.
AWIS ** p
HUNW ** p

Mears, Rick. 1952?- . United
States. Automobile Racing.
SCHA *** p

Mears, Roger. 1947?- . United
States. Automobile Racing.
SCHA *** p

Meggyesy, Dave. 1941- .
United States. Football.
BRIN *** p

Meiffret, José. 1911- . France.
Bicycle Racing.
SPKS *** p

Melton, Bill. [b. William Edwin].
1945- . United States.
Baseball.
HHCR ** p
UHML *** p

Merzario, Arturo. 1943- . Italy.
Automobile Racing.
RACE ** p

Messing, Shep. 1949- . United
States. Soccer.
HROS *** p
MSSS *** p

Meyer, Billy. 1954?- . United
States. Automobile Racing.
SCHA *** p

Meyer, Debbie. [b. Deborah
Elizabeth]. 1952- . United
States. Swimming.
AWIS * p
SOTO ** p

Meyer, Louis. 1904- . United
States. Automobile Racing.
CIND *** p

Meyers, Chief. [b. John Tortes].
1880-1971. United States.
Baseball.
GOTT *** p

Mikan, George Lawrence.
1924-   . United States.
Basketball.
    BBGM ** p
    FPBS ** p
    GSTN ** p
    SPIM ** p

Mikita, Stanley. [b. Stanilas
GVOTH]. 1940-   .
Czechoslovakia. Hockey.
    GCEN ** p/c
    HGAS ** p
    HGST **
    HTSC ** p
    MHSS *** p
    PHHT ** p
    STOH ** p

Miles, Ken. [b. Kenneth Henry].
1918-1966. Great Britain.
Automobile Racing.
    KOMS *** p

Miller, Don. [b. Donald C.].
1902-1979. United States.
Football.
    HUNF * p

Miller, Johnny. 1947-   . United
States. Golf.
    CHCH **
    SSOG *** p

Miller, Kathy. 1964?-   . United
States. Track and Field.
    TTOH *** p

Million Dollar Man. [b. Ted
DiBiase]. Birthdate? United
States. Wrestling.
    WRES ** p

Mills, Billy. 1938-   . United
States. Track and Field.
    AMOS **

Milton, Tommy. [b. Thomas
Willard]. 1894?-1962. United
States. Automobile Racing.
    CIND *** p
    GARD * p
    GMIN ** p

Minton, Greg. [also known as
The Moon Man]. [b. Gregory
Brian]. 1951-   . United States.
Baseball.
    BARP ** p

Missing Link. Birthdate? United
States. Wrestling.
    WRE2 ** p

Mr. Wonderful. [b. Paul
Orndorff]. Birthdate? United
States. Wrestling.
    WRES ** p

Mitchell, Bobby. [b. Robert
Cornelius]. 1935-   . United
States. Football.
    WATT ** p

Mize, John Robert. 1913-   .
United States. Baseball.
    AHRK **

Mizell, Vinegar Bend. [b. Wilmer
David]. 1930-   . United States.
Baseball.
    WATT ** p

Mizerak, Steve. Birthdate?
United States. Pool.
>   BEYD **

Moffitt, Billie Jean see King,
Billie Jean Moffitt

Molineaux, Tom. 1784-   .
United States. Boxing.
>   HWCH ** i
>   POBS ** i

Mo, Little see Connolly, Maureen
Connolly

Monroe, Earl. 1944-   . United
States. Basketball.
>   GSTN ** p
>   PBGR ***

Montana, Joe. [b. Joseph C.].
1956-   . United States. Football.
>   DANF *** p
>   NFLS * p/c
>   SBWL ** p

Montgomery, Wilbert. 1954-   .
United States. Football.
>   FBAB ** p
>   NFLS * p/c

Moody, Helen Wills see Wills,
Helen

Moog, Andy. 1960?-   . Canada.
Hockey.
>   HFGO ** p

Moolah. [also known as The
Fabulous Moolah]. Birthdate?
United States? Wrestling.
>   WRES *

Moon Man, The see Minton, Greg

Moore, Bobby see Rashad,
Ahmad

Moore, Lenny. [b. Leonard
Edward]. 1933-   . United
States. Football.
>   FRRB ** p
>   GRBF *** p
>   GRUN ** p

Morcom, Boo. [b. Richmond].
Birthdate? United States. Track
and Field.
>   BEYD **

Morenz, Howie. [b. Howarth].
1902-1937. Canada. Hockey.
>   FHPL *** p
>   HGST **
>   HHOT *** p
>   STOH ** p

Morgan, George T. Birthdate?
United States. Airplane Racing.
>   MSRS ** p

Morgan, Joe. [b. Joseph
Leonard]. 1943-   . United
States. Baseball.
>   BMVP *** p
>   INFD ** p, p/c
>   LGPS ** p
>   TSBG ** p

Morris, Mercury. [b. Eugene].
1947-   . United States. Football.
>   RUNB ** p, p/c

Morton, Craig L. 1943-   .
United States. Football.
   SQBN *** p

Moser-Proell, Annemarie.
1954?-   . Austria. Skiing.
   WISS ** p

Moses, Edwin. 1955-   . United
States. Track and Field.
   TGCH *** p

Moss, Stirling Crauford.
1929-   . Great Britain.
Automobile Racing.
   CHSP ** i
   SMKR *** p
   WCHP ᴵᵛᴵᵛᴵ p

Mota, Manny. [b. Manuel
Rafael]. 1938-   . Dominican
Republic. Baseball.
   SPSP ** p

Motley, Marion. 1920-   . United
States. Football.
   GRUN ** p
   HUNF * p

Motta, Dick. [b. Richard].
1931-   . United States.
Basketball.
   COAL **

Mount Pleasant, Frank.
Birthdate? United States.
Football.
   GIND ** p

Muldowney, Cha Cha. [b.
Shirley]. 1940?-   . United
States. Automobile Racing.
   MDRS *** p
   WISP *** p

Mulligan, Zookeeper. [b. John].
1943?-1969. United States.
Automobile Racing.
   GARD * p

Mullin, Mo. [b. Chris].
Birthdate? United States.
Basketball.
   YANF ** p

Munoz, Anthony. 1958-   .
United States. Football.
   NFLS * p/c

Munson, Thurman Lee. 1947-
1979. United States. Baseball.
   BMVP *** p
   GBST ** p
   MASK *** p
   TSBG ** p
   UHML ** p

Muraco, Magnificent Don.
Birthdate? United States.
Wrestling.
   WRES ** p

Murcer, Bobby Ray. 1946-   .
United States. Baseball.
   SOML *** p

Murphy, Cal. [b. Calvin].
1948-   . United States.
Basketball.
   LGPS ** p
   ROOK **** p

Murphy, Dale. 1956-   . United
States. Baseball.
    BASS * p/c

Murphy, Isaac. 1861?-1896.
United States. Horse Racing.
    TDTL *** p

Murphy, Jimmy. 1894?-1924.
United States. Automobile
Racing.
    GARD * p

Murphy, John Joseph. 1908-
1970. United States. Baseball.
    TSBG ** p

Murray, Eddie Clarence.
1956-   . United States.
Baseball.
    BASS * p/c

Murtaugh, Dan. [b. Daniel
Edward]. 1917-1976. United
States. Baseball.
    MANG ** p, p/c

Musial, Stan. [also known as
Stan the Man]. [b. Stanley
Frank]. 1920-   . United States.
Baseball.
    AHRK **
    BATA ** p
    BFAM * i
    BIBA **
    BOBG ** p
    BWPL ** p
    GISP ** i
    HOFB ** p
    HUNB ** p
    SMAA ***

TSBG ** p
WATT ** p

Nagurski, Bronko. [b. Bronislau].
1908-   . Canada. Football.
    FBRN *** p
    GISP ** i
    GPRB ** p
    GRUN ** p
    HUNF ** p
    SPIM ** p
    STOF ** p

Namath, Joe. [b. Joseph
William]. 1943-   . United
States. Football.
    ASHT ** p
    BEYD **
    CHCH **
    CHMP ** p/c, i/c
    DANF ** p
    FCQB ** p
    GCIS ** p
    GPQU ** p
    HUNF ** p
    PFHT ** p
    PROQ **** p
    QUAR ** p, p/c
    SBWL ** p
    SPIM ** p
    SQBN *** p
    STOF ** p
    WATT ** p

Nance, Jim. [b. James Solomon].
1942-   . United States. Football.
    GRUN ** p
    SRBN ** p

Nash, Charlie. Birthdate?
Ireland. Boxing.
    BEYD **

Nastase, Ilie. 1946-   . Rumania.
Tennis.
　　FATP *** p

Nater, Swen. 1950-   .
Netherlands. Basketball.
　　GCPB *** p
　　LONH *

Nature Boy. [b. Rick Flair].
Birthdate? United States.
Wrestling.
　　WRES ** p

Navratilova, Martina. 1956-   .
Czechoslovakia. Tennis.
　　FWTP *** p
　　GRLS ** p
　　WWOT ** p

Neilson, Jim. [b. James
Anthony]. 1940-   . Canada.
Hockey.
　　PHHT ** p

Nelsen, Bill. [b. William Keith].
1941-   . United States. Football.
　　SQBN ** p

Nelson, Cindy. [b. Cynthia].
1955-   . United States. Skiing.
　　FMAW *** p
　　MWSS *** p
　　WISS *** p

Nelson, Battling. [b. Oscar].
1882-1954. Denmark. Boxing.
　　POBS ** p

Nettles, Graig. 1944-   . United
States. Baseball.
　　HHCR ** p

Nevers, Ernie. [b. Ernest].
1903-1976. United States.
Football.
　　FRRB ** p
　　GISP ** i
　　GRUN ** p
　　HUNF ** p

Newlin, Mike. 1949-   . United
States. Basketball.
　　BSHP ** p

Newsom, Bobo. [b.Henry Louis].
1907?-   . United States.
Baseball.
　　BZAN *** p

Newsome, Ozzie. 1956-   .
United States. Football
　　FTTE ** p

Nicklaus, Jack William. 1940-   .
United States. Golf.
　　ASHT ** p
　　CHCH **
　　GOGR **** p
　　GOLF **
　　GRLS ** p
　　GTGO *** p
　　SPIM ** p
　　SSOG *** p

Niekro, Phil. [b. Philip Henry].
1939-   . United States.
Baseball.
　　BFIP ** p
　　UHML ** p

Niland, John Hugh. 1944-   .
United States. Football.
　　PFHT ** p

Ning, Li. 1965?- . China.
Gymnastics.
 MLRG ** p

Nitschke, Ray. [b. Raymond
Ernest]. 1936- . United States.
Football.
 QLBN *** p

Nixon, Norm Charles. 1955- .
United States. Basketball.
 BPLM ** p

Nobis, Tommy. [b. Thomas
Henry]. 1943- . United States.
Football.
 GLBN ** p
 LINE ** p, p/c

Noll, Chuck. [b. Charles Henry].
1932- . United States. Football.
 FOCC ** p

Norton, Ken. [b. Kenneth
Howard]. 1945- . United
States. Boxing.
 HWCH ** p

Nurmi, Paavo Johannes. 1897-
1973. Finland. Track and Field.
 GISP ** i
 SOTO **
 SPIM ** p
 TGCH *** p

Nuvolari, Tazio. 1892-1953.
Italy. Automobile Racing.
 CHSP ** i

Nuxhall, Joe. [b. Joseph Henry].
1928- . United States.
Baseball.
 BEYD **

Nyad, Diana. 1949- . United
States. Swimming.
 MMWS *** p
 SXWD ** p
 WSWM ** p
 WWDA ** p, i
 WWOS ** p

O'Brien, Davey. [b. Robert
David]. 1917-1977. United
States. Football.
 HATG **
 HEIS ** p

O'Brien, Parry. [b. William
Parry]. 1932- . United States.
Track and Field.
 TGCH *** p

Ochowicz, Sheila Young see
Young, Sheila

O'Dea, Patrick John. 1873-1962.
Australia. Football.
 HUNF ** p

Odoms, Riley. 1950- . United
States. Football.
 FTTE ** p

O'Doul, Lefty. [b. Francis
Joseph]. 1897-1969. United
States. Baseball.
 GOTT ** p

Oerter, Al. [b. Alfred A].
1936-   . United States. Track
and Field.
    AMOS **
    TGCH *** p

O'Farrell, Bob. [b. Robert
Arthur]. 1896-1988. United
States. Baseball.
    GOTT ** p

Oldfield, Barney. 1878-1946.
United States. Automobile
Racing.
    GARD * p

Oliva, Tony. [b. Antonio Pedro].
1940-   . Cuba. Baseball.
    TSBG ** p

Oliver, Al. [b. Albert]. 1946-   .
United States. Baseball.
    BHOT ** p

Olsen, Merlin. 1940-   . United
States. Football.
    CHMP ** p/c, i/c

O'Neil, Kitty Linn. 1946-   .
United States. Automobile
Racing and Motorcycle Racing.
    SXWD ** p
    TTOH *** p
    WNQT ** p
    WWDA ** p, i
    WWOS ** p

Ongais, Danny. 1940-   . United
States. Automobile Racing.
    GARD ** p

Orndorff, Paul see Mr.
Wonderful

Orr, Bobby. [b. Robert Gordon].
1948-   . Canada. Hockey.
    ASHT ** p
    CHMP ** i/c
    FHPL *** p
    FSWS *** p, i
    GDEF ** p/c
    GRLS ** p
    HGAS ** p
    HGST *** p
    HHOT **** p
    HOPH *** p
    HSSE **
    HTSC ** p
    MHSS *** p
    PHHT ** p
    SPIM ** p
    STOH ** p

Ortega, Gaspar. 1935-   . Mexico.
Boxing.
    GLSF ** p

Ott, Mel. [b. Melvin Thomas].
1909-1958. United States.
Baseball.
    AHRK ***
    BFAM * i
    GISP ** i
    HOFB ** p
    HUNB ** p
    SMAA ****

Ouimet, Francis. 1894-1967.
United States. Golf.
    GOLF ***

Ovett, Steve. 1955- . Great
Britain. Track and Field.
　　TRMM ** p

Owens, Jesse. [b. James
Cleveland]. 1913-1980. United
States. Track and Field.
　　AMOS **
　　AOGL *** p
　　CHOS *** p
　　GISP ** i
　　GRLS ** p
　　SOTO ** p
　　SPIM ** p
　　TGCH *** p

Owens, Steve. [b. Loren Everett].
1947- . United States. Football.
　　GRUN ** p
　　HATG **
　　HEIS ** p

Pace, Carlos. [b. José Carlos].
1944- . Brazil. Automobile
Racing.
　　RACE ** p

Page, Al. [b. Alan Cedric].
1945- . United States. Football.
　　DEFL ** p, p/c
　　GNFL *** p
　　PFHT ** p

Paige, Satchel. [b. Leroy Robert].
1906-1982. United States.
Baseball.
　　BFAM * i
　　BOBG ** p
　　BZAN * p
　　HOFB ** p
　　HUNB ** p
　　PIBB *** p

POBS * p
SPIM ** p

Palmateer, Mike. 1954- .
Canada. Hockey.
　　HFGO ** p

Palmer, Arnold Daniel. 1929- .
United States. Golf.
　　ASHT ** p
　　BEYD **
　　CHCH **
　　GOLF ***
　　GTGO *** p
　　SPIM ** p
　　SSOG *** p

Palmer, Jim. [b. James Alvin].
1945- . United States.
Baseball.
　　BATA ** p
　　BCHP *** p
　　BFIP ** p
　　TSBG ** p

Parent, Bernie. [b. Bernard
Marcel]. 1945- . Canada.
Hockey.
　　GOAL ** p/c
　　MITN ** p
　　PHHT ** p

Park, Brad. [b. Douglas
Bradford]. 1948- . Canada.
Hockey.
　　GDEF ** p/c
　　HSSE **
　　KOTR *** p
　　PHHT ** p

Parker, Dave. [b. David Gene].
1951- . United States.
Baseball.
    BHOT ** p

Parker, Jim. [b. James Thomas].
1934- . United States. Football.
    BEYD **

Parry, Zale. 1933- . United
States. Scuba Diving.
    WSSD ** p

Parsons, Johnnie. 1918- .
United States. Automobile
Racing.
    ARYL ** p

Parsons, Johnny. 1945?-
United States. Automobile
Racing.
    ARYL ** p

Patera, Ken. 1944?- . United
States. Wrestling.
    WRES ** p

Paterno, Joe. [b. Joseph
Vincent]. 1926- . United States.
Football.
    SGFC ** p

Patkin, Max. Birthdate? United
States. Baseball.
    BWPL * p

Patrick, Lester. [b. Curtis
Lester]. 1883-1960. Canada.
Hockey.
    GCIS ** p
    STOH ** p

Patrick, Mike. 1942?- . United
States. Motorcycle Racing.
    DTDD ***

Patterson, Floyd. 1935- .
United States. Boxing.
    AMOS **
    HWCH *** p
    POBS ** p
    SFST ** p
    SOTO **
    WATT ** p

Paultz, Billy. Birthdate? United
States. Basketball.
    LONH ** p

Payne, Nancy. [m. Glasgow].
Birthdate? United States.
Motorcycle Racing.
    WISM ** p

Payton, Sweetness. [b. Walter
Jerry]. 1954- . United States.
Football.
    FBAB ** p
    NFLS * p/c
    RBPS ** p
    STOF ** p

Peach, The Georgia *see* Cobb, Ty

Pearson, David. 1934- . United
States. Automobile Racing.
    DOSW * p
    GARD ** p
    HSCR *** p
    KOMS *** p

Pearson, Drew. 1951- . United
States. Football.
    FSHR ** p

Peck, Annie Smith. 1850-1935.
United States. Mountain
Climbing.
  WWCT *** p
  WWDA ** p, i
  WWOS ** p

Peeters, Pete. 1957- . Canada.
Hockey.
  HFGO ** p

Pelé. [b. Edson Arantes do
Nascimento]. 1940- . Brazil.
Soccer.
  GRLS ** p
  LGPS ** p
  MSSS *** p
  RCHN **
  SPIM ** p

Penske, Captain. [b. Roger].
1937- . United States.
Automobile Racing.
  WGRD ** p

Peoples, Woody. 1943- . United
States. Football.
  CSPS ** p

Pep, Willie. [b. Guiglermo
PAPALEO]. 1922- . United
States. Boxing.
  WATT ** p

Peppler, Mary Jo. 1945?- .
United States. Volleyball.
  HUNW ** p

Perez, Tony. [b. Atanasio Rigal].
1942- . Cuba. Baseball.
  HHCR ** p
  UHML ** p

Perkins, Don. [b. Donald
Anthony]. 1938- . United
States. Football.
  GRBF ** p

Perreault, Gil. [b. Gilbert].
1950- . Canada. Hockey.
  GCEN ** p/c
  HOSS ** p
  HSPH *** p
  HSSE **
  PHHT ** p

Perry, Fred. 1909- . Great
Britain. Tennis.
  FATP *** p

Perry, Gaylord Jackson. 1938- .
United States. Baseball.
  BCHP *** p
  BFIP ** p
  BWPL ** p
  PTCH ** p, p/c

Perry, Joe. [b. Fletcher Joseph].
1927- . United States. Football.
  FRRB ** p
  GRUN ** p

Perry, William. [also known as
The Refrigerator]. 1962- .
United States. Football.
  FOIB ** p

Peterson, Ronnie. 1944- .
Sweden. Automobile Racing.
  RACE ** p

Petrie, Geoff. 1948- . United
States. Basketball.
  HSPB ** p
  ROOK ** p

Petrocelli, Rico. [b. Americo Peter]. 1943-   . United States. Baseball.
    HHCR ** p

Pettit, Bob. [b. Robert E. Lee]. 1932-   . United States. Basketball.
    BBGM ** p
    FPBS ** p
    GSTN *** p

Petty, Lee. 1915-   . United States. Automobile Racing.
    ARYL * p
    GARD * p
    HSCR *** p
    SUPD **** p

Petty, Richard Lee. 1937-   . United States. Automobile Racing.
    ARCD ** p
    ARYL *** p
    DOSW * p
    GARD ** p
    HSCR *** p
    SSAR ** p
    WGRD ** p

Pheidippides [also spelled Philippides]. Birthdate? Greece. Track and Field.
    MARA **
    WCMA **

Phillips, Kristie. Birthdate? United States. Gymnastics.
    YANF ** p

Phillips, Lefty. [b. Harold]. 1919-1972. United States. Baseball.
    COAL ** p

Pidgeon, Harry. 1867?-1954. United States. Sailing.
    SING ** p
    THSA *** p

Piersall, Jim. [b. James Anthony]. 1929-   . United States. Baseball.
    BWPL ** p
    CHOS *** p

Pietri, Dorando. 18____-   . Italy. Track and Field.
    MARA *
    WCMA **

Pilote, Pierre Paul. 1931-   . Canada. Hockey.
    HGST **

Piper, Rowdy Roddy. Birthdate? Great Britain. Wrestling.
    WRES ** p

Pirtle, Sue. 1952?-   . United States. Rodeo.
    WISR ** p

Pitou, Penny. [b. Penelope]. 1938-   . United States. Skiing.
    AWIS **

Plank, Eddie. [b. Edward Stewart]. 1875-1926. United States. Baseball.
    BATA ** p

Plante, Jacques. [b. Joseph
Jacques Omer]. 1929-1986.
Canada. Hockey.
    CHMP ** p/c, i/c
    GGPH *** p
    HGAS ** p
    HGST **
    HHOT *** p
    HMKM *** p, i
    MITN *** p

Player, Gary. 1935?-   . South
Africa. Golf.
    GTGO *** p
    SSOG *** p

Plunkett, Jim. [b. James
William]. 1947-   . United
States. Football.
    CSPS ** p
    GNFL *** p
    HATG **
    HEIS ** p
    PFHT ** p
    SBWL ** p
    WHET ** p

Plunkett, Sherman. 1933-   .
United States. Football.
    FOIB ** p

Pocket Rocket, The *see* Richard,
Henri

Pollard, Art. 1927-1973. United
States. Automobile Racing.
    DOSW * p

Pollard, Fritz. [b. Frederick
Douglas]. 1894-1986. United
States. Football.
    GISP ** i

    HUNF ** p
    POBS ** p
    TDTL ** p

Pont, John. 1927-   . United
States. Football.
    COAL ** p

Porter, Kevin. 1950-   . United
States. Basketball.
    BPLM ** p

Posey, Sam. 1944-   . United
States. Automobile Racing.
    RACE ** p

Post, Dick. [b. Richard M.].
1945-   . United States. Football.
    SRBN ** p

Potvin, Denis Charles. 1953-   .
Canada. Hockey.
    GDEF ** p/c
    HSPH *** p
    KOTR *** p
    MHSS *** p
    SCIH *** p

Powell, Boog. [b. John Wesley].
1941-   . United States.
Baseball.
    GIML ** p
    WATT ** p

Powell, Marvin. 1955-   . United
States. Football.
    FCBL ** p

Prothro, Tommy. [b. James
Thompson]. 1920?-   . United
States. Football.
    COAL ** p

Prudhomme, Snake. [b. Don].
1945?-   . United States.
Automobile Racing.
    MDRS ** p

Prudom, Benjie Bell. Birthdate?
United States. Rodeo.
    WISR ** p

Pruitt, Greg. [b. Gregory
Donald]. 1951-   . United States.
Football.
    FBAB ** p
    LGPS ** p

Pryce, Tom. 1949-   . Great
Britain. Automobile Racing.
    RACE ** p

Puckett, Kirby. 1961-   . United
States. Baseball.
    BHNS *** p

Quisenberry, Dan. [b. Daniel
Raymond]. 1953-   . United
States. Baseball.
    BARP ** p
    BASS * p/c

Rader, Doug. [b. Douglas Lee].
1944-   . United States.
Baseball.
    BWPL ** p
    HHCR ** p
    UHML ** p

Ramsey, Frank. 1931-   . United
States. Basketball.
    THCF ** p

Rankin, Judy. [b. Judith
TORLUEMKE]. 1945-   . United
States. Golf.
    MWSS *** p

Rashad, Ahmad. [b. Bobby
Moore]. 1949-   . United States.
Football.
    FSHR ** p

Ratelle, Jean. 1940-   . Canada.
Hockey.
    UFTM *** p

Rayborn, Calvin. 1940-   .
United States. Motorcycle
Racing.
    SPKS *** p

Redman, Brian. 1937-   . Great
Britain. Automobile Racing.
    RACE ** p

Redmond, Mickey. [b. Michael
Edward]. 1947-   . Canada.
Hockey.
    HSSE **
    PHHT ** p

Red Rooster. [b. Terry Taylor].
Birthdate? United States.
Wrestling.
    WRE2 ** p

Reed, Willis. 1942-   . United
States. Basketball.
    BBGM ** p
    CHMP ** p/c, i/c
    GCIS * p
    GIFC ****
    GSTN ** p
    LONH *** p

Reel, Chi Cheng *see* Cheng, Chi

Reese, Pee Wee. [b. Harold
Henry]. 1918-   . United States.
Baseball.
    GIML ** p

Refrigerator, The *see* Perry,
William

Regazzoni, Clay. [b.
Gianclaudio]. 1939-   .
Switzerland. Automobile Racing.
    RACE ** p

Reid, Mike. [b. Michael B].
1948-   . United States. Football.
    FSSS *** p

Reiser, Pete. [b. Harold Patrick].
1919-1981. United States.
Baseball.
    CHOS *** p

Rentzel, Lance. [b. T. Lance].
1943-   . United States. Football.
    BEYD **

Resch, Chico. [b. Glenn].
1948-   . Canada. Hockey.
    HFGO ** p

Resweber, Carroll. 1936-   .
United States. Motorcycle
Racing.
    DTDD ***

Retton, Mary Lou. 1968-   .
United States. Gymnastics.
    MLRG *** p

Reutemann, Carlos. 1942-   .
Argentina. Automobile Racing.
    RACE ** p

Revson, Peter Jeffrey. 1939?-
1974. United States. Automobile
Racing.
    DOSW ** p
    SSAR ** p

Rhodes, Dusty. Birthdate?
United States. Wrestling.
    WRES ** p

Rice, Jim. [b. James Edward].
1953-   . United States.
Baseball.
    BAPH ** p

Richard, Henri. [also known as
The Pocket Rocket]. 1936-   .
Canada. Hockey.
    FHPL *** p

Richard, Rocket. [b. Maurice].
1921-   . Canada. Hockey.
    FHPL *** p
    HGAS ** p
    HGST **
    HHOT *** p
    HOPH *** p
    HTSC ** p
    RBPS ** p
    SPIM ** p
    STOH ** p

Richter, Wendi. Birthdate?
United States. Wrestling.
    WRES * p

Rickenbacker, Eddie. [b. Edward Vernon]. 1890-1973. United States. Automobile Racing.
GARD ** p

Rickey, Branch. [b. Wesley Branch]. 1881-1965. United States. Baseball.
BFAM * i
CHOS *** p
HUNB ** p
POBS **

Rigby, Cathy. [m. Mason]. 1952- . United States. Gymnastics.
CWSP *
GOLG ** p
HUNW ** p
WIGY ** p
WISP *** p
WOWW *** p

Riggins, John. 1949- . United States. Football.
FBAB ** p
GRUN ** p

Riggs, Bobby. [b. Robert Larimore]. 1918- . United States. Tennis.
FATP *** p

Rindt, Karl-Jochen. 1942-1970. West Germany. Automobile Racing.
WCHP *** p

Ripken, Cal. [b. Calvin Edwin Jr]. 1960- . United States. Baseball.
BASS * p/c

Rivers, David. Birthdate? United States. Basketball.
YANF ** p

Rizzuto, Phil [also known as Scooter]. [b. Philip Francis.] 1918- . United States. Baseball.
GIML ** p

Roark, Helen Wills Moody *see* Wills, Helen

Roberts, Fireball. [b. Edward Glenn]. 1929-1964. United States. Automobile Racing.
GARD ** p
HSCR ** p

Roberts, Jake the Snake. [b. Jake]. Birthdate? United States. Wrestling.
WRE2 ** p

Roberts, Robin Evan. 1926- . United States. Baseball.
BIBA ***

Robertson, Isiah. Birthdate? United States. Football.
MSLB ** p, p/c

Robertson, Oscar Palmer. 1938- . United States. Basketball.
BSTG *** p
CHMP ** i/c
FPBS ** p
GSTN ** p
WATT ** p

Robeson, Paul LeRoy. 1898-
1976. United States. Football.
    HUNF ** p

Robinson, Brooks Calbert.
1937- . United States.
Baseball.
    BATA ** p
    BFAM * i
    CHMP ** p/c, i/c
    GAML **
    GIML ** p
    HHCR *** p
    HUNB ** p
    INFD ** p, p/c
    SMAA ***
    TSBG ** p

Robinson, Dave. [b. Richard
David]. 1941- . United States.
Football.
    LINE ** p, p/c
    QLBN ** p

Robinson, David Maurice.
1965- . United States.
Basketball.
    YANF ** p

Robinson, Frank. 1935- .
United States. Baseball.
    AHRK **
    ASHT ** p
    MANG ** p, p/c
    TSBG ** p

Robinson, Jackie. [b. Jack
Roosevelt]. 1919-1972. United
States. Baseball.
    BEYD **

    BFAM * i
    BIBA ***
    BOBG ** p
    BRIN *** p
    CHOS *** p
    GBST *** p
    GIML *** p
    GISP ** i
    GRLS ** p
    HHCR ** p
    HOFB ** p
    HUNB ** p
    PIBB *** p
    POBS ** p
    SHWQ *** p
    TDTL *** p
    TSBG ** p

Robinson, Paul. Birthdate?
United States. Football.
    GRBF ** p

Robinson, Sugar Ray. [b. Walker
Smith, Jr.]. 1921-1989. United
States. Boxing.
    POBS ** p
    SPIM ** p

Robinson, Wilbert. 1864-1934.
United States. Baseball.
    BGMA ** p
    HUNB ** p

Rocca, Argentina. [b. Antonino].
1923-1977. Italy. Wrestling.
    WRES ** p

Rocket, The Pocket *see* Richard,
Henri

Rocketman, The *see* Gary
Gabelich

Rockne, Knute Kenneth. 1888-
1931. Norway. Football.
    GISP ** i
    HUNF ** p
    SGFC ** p
    STOF ** p

Rodgers, Bill. 1947- . United
States. Track and Field.
    MARA ** p
    WCMA ** p

Rodgers, Johnny. 1951- .
United States. Football.
    HATG *** p
    HEIS ** p

Rodnina, Irina. 1949- . Union
of Soviet Socialist Republics. Ice
Skating.
    WOTI ** p

Rodriguez, Aurelio. 1947- .
Mexico. Baseball.
    HHCR ** p

Rodriguez, Chi-Chi. [b. Juan].
1935- . Puerto Rico. Golf.
    BEYD **
    GLSF *** p

Rogers, George Washington Jr.
1958- . United States. Football.
    HATG **
    NFLS * p/c

Rojas, Cookie. [b. Octavio Rivas].
1939- . Cuba. Baseball.
    UHML ** p

Rooster, Red *see* Red Rooster

Rose, Alec. 1908- . Great
Britain. Sailing.
    SING ** p

Rose, Doug. Birthdate? United
States. Automobile Racing.
    MSRS *** p

Rose, Mauri. 1906- . United
States. Automobile Racing.
    CIND *** p
    GARD ** p
    GMIN **

Rose, Pete. [also known as
Charley Hustle]. [b. Peter
Edward]. 1941- . United
States. Baseball.
    ASHT ** p
    BASS * p/c
    BEYD **
    BHOT ** p
    CAPS *** p
    HITT ** p, p/c
    RBPS ** p
    SOSW *** p
    TSBG ** p

Rosendahl, Heidemarie. [m.
Ecker]. 1947- . West Germany.
Track and Field.
    HUNW ** p

Rosewall, Ken. 1934- .
Australia. Tennis.
    TENN **

Ross, Barney. [b. Barnet David
RASOFSKY]. 1909-1967. United
States. Boxing.
  CHOS *** p
  GLTR *** p

Rossovich, Tim. [b. Timothy J].
1946- . United States. Football.
  PFHT ** p

Rote, Kyle Jr. 1950- . United
States. Soccer.
  HROS *** p
  MSSS *** p

Roth, Joe. ?-1977. United
States. Football.
  SUSS ** p

Roth, Werner. 1948- .
Yugoslavia. Soccer.
  MSSS *** p

Rotundo, Mike. Birthdate?
United States. Wrestling.
  WRES ** p

Roundfield, Dan. 1953- .
United States. Basketball.
  BAPP ** p

Roush, Edd J. 1893-1988.
United States. Baseball.
  GOTT *** p

Roussimoff, Andrae Rene *see*
André the Giant

Royal, Darrell K. 1924- .
United States. Football.
  COAL ** p

Rozelle, Pete. [b. Alvin Ray].
1926- . United States.
Football [commissioner].
  CHCH **

Rozier, Mike. 1961- . United
States. Football.
  HATG **

Rubin, Barbara Jo. 1949- .
United States. Horse Racing.
  AWIS * p

Rude, Ravishing Rick.
Birthdate? United States.
Wrestling.
  WRE2 **

Rudi, Joe. [b. Joseph Oden].
1946- . United States.
Baseball.
  UHML ** p

Rudolph, Wilma. [also known as
Skeeter]. 1940- . United States.
Track and Field.
  AMOS **
  AWIS ** p
  CWSP *** p
  GISP ** i
  GOLG ** p
  HUNW ** p
  SOTO ** p
  TRGW ** p
  WWOS ** p

Ruffin, Nate. Birthdate? United
States. Football.
  BEYD **

Ruland, Jeff. 1958-   . United
States. Basketball.
    BAPP ** p

Russell, Andy. [b. Charles
Andrew]. 1941-   . United States.
Football.
    BEYD **

Russell, Bill. [b. William
Fenton]. 1934-   . United States.
Basketball.
    ASHT ** p
    BBGM ** p
    COAL ** p
    FPBS ** p
    GRLS ** p
    GSTN *** p
    LONH *** p
    PBBM **** p
    SPIM ** p
    TDTL *** p
    THCF ** p

Russell, Cazzie. 1944-   . United
States. Basketball.
    GCIS * p

Ruth, Babe. [b. George Herman].
1895-1948. United States.
Baseball.
    AHRK ***
    BATA ** p
    BFAM * i
    BGSL *** p
    BHRH ** p
    BIBA ***
    BOBG ** p
    GAML ***
    GBST ** p
    GISP ** i
    GRLS ** p

HOFB ** p
HOHR ** p
HUNB ** p
PIBB *** p
SMAA ***
SPIM ** p
TSBG ** p

Ryan, Nolan. [b. Lynn Nolan].
1947-   . United States.
Baseball.
    BFIP ** p
    GBST ** p
    PTCH ** p, p/c
    RBPS ** p

Ryun, Jim. [b. James Ronald].
1947-   . United States. Track
and Field.
    ASHT ** p
    BEYD **
    GISP ** i
    SOTO ** p
    SPKS *** p
    TRMM ** p

Saberhagen, Bret William.
1964-   . United States.
Baseball.
    BASS * p/c
    BHNS *** p

Sachs, Eddie. [b. Edward Julius].
1927-1964. United States.
Automobile Racing.
    GARD ** p
    KOMS *** p

Saddler, Sandy. [b. Joseph].
1926-   . United States. Boxing.
    POBS ** p

Salazar, Alberto. 1958-   . Cuba.
Track and Field.
    WCMA ** p

Sammartino, Bruno. 1937?-   .
Italy. Wrestling.
    BEYD **
    WRES ** p

Sandberg, Ryne Dee. 1959-   .
United States. Baseball.
    BASS * p/c

Sanders, Charles A. 1946-   .
United States. Football.
    FTTE ** p
    SPRN *** p

Sanders, Satch. [b. Thomas E.].
1938-   . United States.
Basketball.
    THCF ** p

Sanderson, Turk. [b. Derek
Michael]. 1946-   . Canada.
Hockey.
    GFAW ***
    HSSE ***

Saneyev, Viktor. 1945-   . Union
of Soviet Socialist Republics.
Track and Field.
    TGCH ** p

Sanguillen, Manny. [b. Manuel].
1944-   . Panama. Baseball.
    CACH ** p, p/c

Santana, Tito. Birthdate?
Mexico. Football and Wrestling.
    WRE2 ** p

Santee, David. 1957-   . United
States. Ice Skating.
    STOI ** p

Santee, James. Birthdate?
United States. Ice Skating.
    STOI ** p

Santo, Ron. [b. Ronald Edward].
1940-   . United States.
Baseball.
    HHCR ** p

Sarazon, Gene. [b. Eugene].
1901?-   . United States. Golf.
    GOLF ***

Sardinias, Eligio. [also known as
Kid Chocolate]. 1907-   . Cuba.
Boxing.
    POBS ** p

Saudan, Sylvain. Birthdate?
Switzerland. Skiing.
    WOSS ** p

Sauer, George H. Jr. Birthdate?
United States. Football.
    BEYD **
    GPCP *** p

Savage, Randy *see* Macho Man

Sawchuk, Terry. [b. Terrance
Gordon]. 1929-1970. Canada.
Hockey.
    FHPL *** p
    GGPH *** p
    HGAS ** p
    HGST **
    HHOT *** p
    HMKM **** p, i

MITN *** p

Sayers, Gale Eugene. 1943-   .
United States. Football.
  ASHT ** p
  BEYD **
  CHMP ** i/c
  FBRN **** p
  FRRB ** p
  GPRB ** p
  GRBF ** p
  GRUN ** p
  HUNF ** p
  SRBN ** p

Say Hey Kid, The *see* Mays,
Willie Howard

Schaefer, Germany. [b. Herman
A]. 1878-1919. United States.
Baseball.
  BWPL *
  BZAN **

Schaus, Frederick. 1925-   .
United States. Basketball.
  COAL ** p

Schayes, Dolph. [b. Adolph].
1928-   . United States.
Basketball.
  BBGM ** p
  FPBS ** p
  GSTN *** p

Scheckter, Jody. 1950-   . South
Africa. Automobile Racing.
  RACE ** p
  SSAR ** p

Schmeling, Max. 1905-   . West
Germany. Boxing.
  SFST ** p

Schmidt, Kathy. 1953-   . United
States. Track and Field.
  WSTF ** p

Schmidt, Mike. [b. Michael
Jack]. 1949-   . United States.
Baseball.
  BAPH ** p
  TSBG ** p

Schmidt, Milton Conrad.
1918-   . Canada. Hockey.
  HGST **

Schoendienst, Red. [b. Albert
Fred]. 1923-   . United States.
Baseball.
  SHWQ *** p

Schollander, Don. [b. Donald
Arthur]. 1946-   . United States.
Swimming.
  ASHT ** p
  BRIN *** p
  SOTO **

Schultz, Dave. 1949-   . Canada.
Hockey.
  GWNG ** p/c

Score, Herb. [b. Herbert Jude].
1933-   . United States.
Baseball.
  GIFC ***

Scott, Charlie. 1948-   . United
States. Basketball.
  UHPB *** p

Scott, George. 1944-   . United
States. Baseball.
  HHCR **
  OTWU ** p

Scott, Jake. [b. Jacob E. III].
1945-   . United States. Football.
  SBWL ** p

Sears, Eleo. [b. Eleanora]. 1881-
1968. United States. Horseback
Riding.
  AWIS ** p
  CWSP *
  HUNW ** p

Seaver, Tom. [b. George
Thomas]. 1944-   . United
States. Baseball.
  BATA ** p
  BCHP ** p
  BEYD **
  BFIP ** p
  CHMP ** i/c
  MOBS ** p
  PTCH ** p, p/c
  RBML ** p
  SPML *** p

Seibert, Michael. 1960?-   .
United States. Ice Skating.
  STOI * p

Seikaly, Rony. Birthdate?
Greece. Basketball.
  YANF ** p

Selmon, Lee Roy. 1954-   .
United States. Football.
  FPPR ** p
  NFLS * p/c

Shank, Theresa. 1951?-   .
United States. Basketball.
  WISP *** p

Sharkey, Jack. [b. Paul Josef
CUKOSCHAY]. 1902-   . United
States. Boxing.
  SFST * p

Sharman, Bill. [b. William].
1926-   . United States.
Basketball.
  COAA ** p/c
  COAL ** p
  THCF ** p

Shaw, Wilbur. [b. Warren
Wilbur]. 1902-1954. United
States. Automobile Racing.
  CIND *** p
  GARD * p
  GMIN **
  SPIM ** p

Shea, Julie. 1959-   . United
States. Track and Field.
  SWTR *** p

Sheik, Iron see Iron Sheik, The

Shelby, Carroll. 1923-   . United
States. Automobile Racing.
  GARD **

Shelley, Ken. Birthdate? United
States. Ice Skating.
  STOI ** p

Shoemaker, Willie. [b. Billy Lee].
1931-   . United States. Horse
Racing.
  SPIM ** p

Shore, Edward William. 1902-
1985. Canada. Hockey.
  HGAS *** p
  HGST **
  STOH ** p
  UFTM *** p

Shorter, Frank. 1947-   . United
States. Track and Field.
  MARA *** p
  SOTO **
  WCMA ** p

Shula, Don. [b. Donald Francis].
1930-   . United States. Football.
  COAH ** p, p/c
  FOCC ** p
  SGFC **
  STOF * p

Shuman, Ron. Birthdate? United
States. Automobile Racing.
  SCHA *** p

Siemon, Jeff. [b. Jeffrey G].
1950-   . United States. Football.
  LINE ** p, p/c
  MSLB ** p, p/c

Siki, Battling. [b. Louis PHAL].
1897-1925. Senegal. Boxing.
  POBS ** p

Sikma, Jack. 1955-   . United
States. Basketball.
  BAPP ** p

Silas, James. 1949-   . United
States. Basketball.
  CSPS ** p

Simburg, Wyomia Tyus *see* Tyus,
Wyomia

Simmons, Al. [b. Aloysius
Harry]. 1902-1956. United
States. Baseball.
  BIBA ***

Simmons, Ted Lyle. 1949-   .
United States. Baseball.
  CACH ** p, p/c
  MASK ** p

Simpson, O. J. [b. Orenthal
James]. 1947-   . United States.
Football.
  ANFL *** p
  ASHT ** p
  FBAB ** p
  FSSS *** p
  GPRB ** p
  GRUN ** p
  HATG *** p
  HEIS ** p
  PFHT ** p
  RBPS ** p
  RUNB ** p, p/c
  SRBN ** p
  STOF ** p
  WATT ** p
  WHET ** p

Sims, Billy. 1955-   . United
States. Football.
  HATG **
  NFLS * p/c

Sinkwich, Frank. [b. Francis].
1920-   . United States. Football.
  HATG **
  HEIS ** p

Sisler, George Harold. 1893-
1973. United States. Baseball.
  BFAM * i
  GAML **
  HOFB ** p
  HUNB ** p

Sittler, Darryl Glen. 1950- .
Canada. Hockey.
  KOTR ** p

Skeeter *see* Rudolph, Wilma

Skowron, Bill. [also known as
Moose]. [b. William Joseph].
1930- . United States.
Baseball.
  WATT ** p

Slack, Mike. Birthdate? United
States. Track and Field.
  MARA **

Slaney, Mary Decker *see* Decker,
Mary

Slaughter, Sargeant. [b. Robert].
Birthdate? United States.
Wrestling.
  WRES ** p

Sloan, Jerry. 1942- . United
States. Basketball.
  PBGR **

Slocum, Joshua. 1844-1909?.
Canada. Sailing.
  SING ** p
  THSA *** p

Smith, Billy. 1950- . Canada.
Hockey.
  HFGO ** p

Smith, Bruce. 1920-1967.
United States. Football.
  HATG **
  HEIS ** p

Smith, Bubba. [b. Charles
Aaron]. 1945- . United States.
Football.
  DEFL ** p, p/c
  FOIB ** p

Smith, Elmore. Birthdate?
United States. Basketball.
  LONH ** p

Smith, Ozzie. [b. Osborne Earl].
1954- . United States.
Baseball.
  BASS * p/c

Smith, Robyn Caroline.
1944?- . United States. Horse
Racing.
  WISP ** p

Smith, Stacy. Birthdate? United
States. Ice Skating.
  STOI ** p

Smythe, Conn Stafford. 1895-
1980. Canada. Hockey.
  STOH ** p

Snead, Sam. [b. Samuel
Jackson]. 1912- . United
States. Golf.
  GOLF ***

Snell, Matt. [b. Matthew].
1941-   . United States. Football.
  GRUN ** p
  SRBN *

Snell, Peter. 1938-   . New
Zealand. Track and Field.
  TGCH *** p

Sneva, Tom. [b. Thomas Edsol].
1948-   . United States.
Automobile Racing.
  DOSW ** p

Snider, Duke. [b. Edwin Donald].
1926-   . United States.
Baseball.
  AHRK **
  BFAM * i

Snively, Mike. Birthdate? United
States? Automobile Racing.
  KOMS **

Snodgrass, Snow. [b. Fred
Carlisle]. 1887-1974. United
States. Baseball.
  GOTT **** p

Snuka, Jimmy *see* Superfly

Sockalexis, Louis. 1873-1913.
United States. Baseball.
  PIBB ** p

Soutar, Judy Cook. 1944-   .
United States. Bowling.
  FMAW ** p

Spahn, Warren Edward.
1921-   . United States.
Baseball.
  BIBA ***
  HOFB ** p
  HUNB ** p

Spalding, A. G. [b. Albert
Goodwill]. 1850-1915. United
States. Baseball.
  PIBB *** p

Speaker, Spoke. [b. Tristram E.].
1888-1958. United States.
Baseball.
  BFAM * i
  GAML **
  HOFB ** p
  HOHR *** p
  HUNB ** p
  TSBG ** p

Sperber, Paula. 1951-   . United
States. Bowling.
  WOWW *** p

Spitz, Mark Andrew. 1950-   .
United States. Swimming.
  AMOS **
  SOTO ** p
  SPKS *** p

Spock, Benjamin. 1903-   .
United States. Rowing.
  AOGL *** p

Spurrier, Steve. [b. Stephen
Orr]. 1945-   . United States.
Football.
  HATG **
  HEIS ** p

Stabler, Ken Michael. 1945- .
United States. Football.
  FWQB ** p

Stagg, Amos Alonzo. 1862-1965.
United States. Football.
  HUNF ** p
  SGFC *** p
  STOF ** p

Stallworth, John. 1952- .
United States. Football.
  FSHR ** p

Stanhouse, Don. [b. Donald
Joseph]. 1951- . United States.
Baseball.
  BWPL ** p

Stan the Man see Musial, Stan

Starbuck, Jo Jo. 1951?- .
United States. Ice Skating.
  STOI ** p

Stargell, Willie. [b. Wilver
Dornel]. 1940- . United States.
Baseball.
  BAPH ** p

Starr, Bart. [b. Bryan Bartlett].
1934- . United States. Football.
  FCQB ** p
  GPQU ** p
  PROQ *** p
  QUAR ** p, p/c
  SBWL *** p

Stasiuk, Vic. [b. Victor John].
1929- . Canada. Hockey.
  COAL ** p

Stastny, Peter. 1956- .
Czechoslovakia. Hockey.
  HOSS ** p

Staubach, Roger. 1942- .
United States. Football.
  CAPS *** p
  DANF *** p
  FSWS *** p, i
  FWQB ** p
  HATG *** p
  HEIS ** p
  QUAR ** p, p/c
  SBWL ** p
  STOF ** p
  WHET ** p

Steamboat, Rick see Dragon

Stecher, Renate Meissner.
1950- . East Germany. Track
and Field.
  TRGW *** p

Steele, George see Animal, The

Stenersen, Johanna. 1959?- .
United States. Motorcycle
Racing.
  WISM ** p

Stenerud, Jan. 1943- . Norway.
Football.
  GNFL *** p

Stengel, Casey. [b. Charles
Dillon]. 1889-1975. United
States. Baseball.
  BABM ** p
  BEYD **
  BFAM * i

BGMA *** p
BWPL ** p
BZAN *** p
COAL *
HOFB ** p
HUNB ** p
SGBM *** p
TSBG ** p

Stewart, Jackie. [b. John Young].
1939-   . Great Britain.
Automobile Racing.
    BEYD **
    CHSP ** i
    IRCD ** p, p/c
    SMKR *** p
    SSAR ** p
    WCHP *** p
    WGRD *** p

Still, Art. [b. Arthur Barry].
1955-   . United States. Football.
    FPPR ** p

Stingley, Darryl. 1951-   .
United States. Football.
    SUSS ** p

Stone, Steve. [b. Steven
Michael]. 1947-   . United
States. Baseball.
    CSPS ** p

Stoneham, Horace. 1904-   .
United States. Baseball [owner].
    CHCH **

Strawberry, Darryl Eugene.
1962-   . United States.
Baseball.
    BASS * p/c
    BHNS *** p

Street, Adrian. Birthdate? Great
Britain. Wrestling.
    WRES ** p

Strickland, Shirley. [m. de la
Hunty]. 1925-   . Australia.
Track and Field.
    TRGW ** p

Strong, Ken. [b. Elmer Kenneth].
1906-   . United States. Football.
    GRUN ** p
    HUNF ** p

Stuck, Hans Joachim. 1951-   .
West Germany. Automobile
Racing.
    RACE ** p

Studd, Big John see Big John
Studd

Stuhldreher, Harry. 1901-1965.
United States. Football.
    HUNF * p

Sullivan, John Lawrence. [also
known as Boston Strong Boy].
1858-1918. United States.
Boxing.
    BHCF * i
    BHWC ** p, i
    HWCH ** p, i
    SFST ** p, i

Sullivan, Pat [b. Patrick Joseph].
1950-   . United States. Football.
    HATG **
    HEIS ** p

Summers, John. Birthdate?
United States. Ice Skating.
    STOI ** p

Summers, Bob. [b. Robert
Sherman]. 1937?- . United
States. Automobile Racing.
    MSRS *** p

Sunday, Billy. [b. William
Ashley]. 1862-1935. United
States. Baseball.
    HUNB ** p

Superfly. [b. Jimmy Snuka].
Birthdate? United States.
Wrestling.
    WRES ** p

Surtees, John. 1934- . Great
Britain. Automobile Racing.
    GCIS ** p
    SMKR ***
    WCHP *** p

Sutter, Bruce. [b. Howard
Bruce]. 1953- . United States.
Baseball.
    BARP ** p
    BFIP ** p
    TSBG ** p

Swann, Lynn Curtis. 1952- .
United States. Football.
    FSHR ** p
    SBWL ** p

Switzer, Kathy. [b. Kathrine].
1947- . United States. Track
and Field.
    BEYD **

Syedikh, Yuriy. 1955- . Union
of Soviet Socialist Republics.
Track and Field.
    TGCH ** p

Szabo, Ekaterina. 1966- .
Rumania. Gymnastics.
    MLRG * p

Szewinska, Irena Kirszenstein.
1946- . Union of Soviet
Socialist Republics. Track and
Field.
    TRGW *** p

Talbert, Billy. [b. William
Franklin]. 1918- . United
States. Tennis.
    CTTC ** p

Tallon, Dale. [b. Michael Dale].
1950- . Canada. Hockey.
    HSSE **

Tanner, Sammy. 1937?- .
United States. Automobile
Racing.
    KOMS ** p

Tarkenton, Fran. [b. Francis
Asbury]. 1940- . United States.
Football.
    DANF *** p
    FWQB ** p
    QUAR ** p, p/c
    STOF * p

Tatum, Jack. [b. John David].
1948- . United States. Football.
    FSSS *** p

Taylor, Bruce Lawrence.
1948-   . United States. Football.
    GNFL *** p

Taylor, Charles R. 1941-   .
United States. Football.
    GPCP *** p
    RECS ** p, p/c
    WATT ** p

Taylor, Jim. [b. James Charles].
1935-   . United States. Football.
    GPRB ** p
    GRBF *** p
    GRUN ** p

Taylor, Larry. [b. Lawrence].
1959-   . United States. Football.
    FHHL ** p
    NFLS * p/c

Taylor, Lee. ?-1980. United
States. Boat Racing.
    MSRS *** p

Taylor, Otis. 1942-   . United
States. Football.
    GPCP *** p
    PFHT ** p
    RECS ** p, p/c
    SPRN *** p

Taylor, Terry *see* Red Rooster

Taylor, Valerie. 1936-   .
Australia. Scuba Diving.
    WSSD *** p

Tekulve, Ken. [b. Kenton
Charles]. 1947-   . United States.
Baseball.
    BARP ** p

Tenace, Gene. [b. Fiore Gino].
1946-   . United States.
Baseball.
    BEYD **
    RBML ** p

Terry, Bill. [b. William Harold].
1898-   . United States.
Baseball.
    BATA ** p
    SMAA **

Testaverde, Vinny. [b. Vincent
Frank]. 1963-   . United States.
Football.
    YANF ** p

Tewanima, Lou. [b. Louis]. ?-
1969. United States. Track and
Field.
    GIND *** p

Theismann, Joe. [b. Joseph
Robert]. 1949-   . United States.
Football.
    DANF *** p
    NFLS * p/c

Thesz, Lou. Birthdate? United
States. Wrestling.
    WRES *

Thomas, Debi. 1967?-   . United
States. Ice Skating.
    YANF ** p

Thomas, Duane. 1947-   . United
States. Football.
    SRBN ** p

Thomas, Gorman. [b. James
Gorman]. 1950- . United
States. Baseball.
    BAPH ** p

Thomas, Pat Calvin. 1954- .
United States. Football.
    FDDB ** p

Thompson, Daley. [b. Francis
Morgan]. 1958- . Great Britain.
Track and Field.
    TGCH *** p

Thompson, Dannie. Birthdate?
United States. Automobile
Racing.
    ARYL * p

Thompson, David. 1954- .
United States. Basketball.
    BHFL ** p
    FORW ** p/c

Thompson, Mickey. 1928- .
United States. Automobile
Racing.
    ARYL *** p
    GARD ** p
    KOMS *** p

Thomson, Johnny. 1922-1960.
United States. Automobile
Racing.
    DTDD ***

Thomson, Peter. 1929- .
Australia. Golf.
    GTGO *** p

Thomson, Bobby. [b. Robert
Brown]. 1923- . Great Britain.
Baseball.
    WATT ** p

Thorpe, Jim. [b. James Francis].
1888-1953. United States.
Football and Track and Field.
    BEYD **
    FRRB ** p
    GIND *** p
    GISP ** i
    GPRB ** p
    GRLS ** p
    GRUN ** p
    HUNF ** p
    SOTO ** p
    SPIM ** p
    STOF ** p

Throneberry, Marvin Eugene.
1933- . United States.
Baseball.
    BWPL *

Thurman, Sammy Fancher.
Birthdate? United States. Rodeo.
    WISR ** p

Thurmond, Nate. 1941- .
United States. Basketball.
    LONH *** p

Tiant, Luis Clemente. 1940- .
Cuba. Baseball.
    BFIP ** p

Tickner, Charles. 1953- .
United States. Ice Skating.
    STOI ** p
    WOTI ** p

Tilden, Bill. [b. William Tatem].
1893-1953. United States.
Tennis.
    CTTC ** p
    FATP *** p
    TENN **
    SPIM ** p
    WMOT ** p

Tinker, Joe. [b. Joseph Bert].
1880-1948. United States.
Baseball.
    HUNB * p

Tittle, Y. A. [b. Yelberton
Abraham]. 1926-   . United
States. Football.
    FCQB ** p
    GCIS ** p
    GIFC ****
    GPQU ** p
    HUNF ** p

Tkaczuk, Walter Robert.
1947-   . Canada. Hockey.
    HSSE ***

Toomey, Bill. [b. William
Anthony]. 1939-   . United
States. Track and Field.
    SOTO *** p

Toporcer, Specs. [b. George].
1899-1989. United States.
Baseball.
    GOTT ** p

Torluemke, Judy see Rankin,
Judy

Torre, Joe. [b. Joseph Paul.]
1940-   . United States.
Baseball.
    GCML *** p
    HHCR ** p
    MASK ** p

Toussaint, Cheryl. 1952-   .
United States. Track and Field.
    WOWW *** p

Trafton, George. 1896-1971.
United States. Football.
    HUNF * p

Train, The Big see Johnson,
Barney

Traynor, Pie. [b. Harold Joseph].
1899-1972. United States.
Baseball.
    BATA ** p
    HHCR **
    HOFB ** p
    HUNB ** p
    SMAA ***
    TSBG ** p

Tremblay, J. C. [b. Jean Claude].
1939-   . Canada. Hockey.
    PHHT ** p

Tretiak, Vladislav. 1952-   .
Union of Soviet Socialist
Republics. Hockey.
    GGPH *** p

Trevino, Lee Buck. 1939- .
United States. Golf.
    GLSF ** p
    GOGR **** p
    SSOG ** p
    WNQT ** p

Triplett, Ernie. 1906-1934.
United States. Automobile
Racing.
    DTDD **

Trippi, Charles Louis. 1922- .
United States. Football.
    GRUN ** p
    HUNF ** p

Trost, Al. 1949- . United
States. Soccer.
    MSSS *** p

Trottier, Bryan. 1956- .
Canada. Hockey.
    HOSS ** p

Tsukahara, Mitsuo. 1947- .
Japan. Gymnastics.
    WIGY ** p

Tucker, Bob. [b. Robert Louis].
1945- . United States.
Football.
    FSSS *** p

Tunnell, Emlen. 1925-1975.
United States. Football.
    HUNF ** p

Tunney, Gene. [b. James
Joseph]. 1898-1978. United
States. Boxing.
    BHWC ** p
    HWCH ** p
    SFST ** p

Turcotte, Ron. 1941- . Canada.
Horse Racing.
    GFAW ***

Turley, Bob. [b. Robert Lee].
1930- . United States.
Baseball.
    WATT ** p

Turner, Bulldog. [b. Clyde].
1919- . United States. Football.
    GLBN ** p
    HUNF ** p

Turner, Pops. [b. Curtis]. 1924-
1970. United States. Automobile
Racing.
    GARD * p
    HSCR ** p

Turton, Janene. 1954?- .
United States. Motorcycle
Racing.
    WISM ** p

Tyson, Mike. 1966- . United
States. Boxing.
    YANF *** p

Tyus, Wyomia. [m. Simburg].
1945- . United States. Track
and Field.
    CWSP *
    GOLG ** p
    HUNW ** p

TRGW ** p
WISP *** p

Uecker, Bob. [b. Robert George].
1935-   . United States.
Baseball.
    BWPL **

Ullman, Norman Victor.
1935-   . Canada. Hockey.
    HGST ** p

Uncle Elmer. Birthdate? United
States. Wrestling.
    WRE2 **

Unger, Garry Douglas. 1947-   .
Canada. Hockey.
    HSSE **
    PHHT ** p

Unitas, Johnny. [b. John
Constantine]. 1933-   . United
States. Football.
    ASHT ** p
    CHMP ** i/c
    CHOS *** p
    DANF ** p
    FCQB ** p
    GCIS ** p
    GISP ** i
    GPQU ** p
    GRLS ** p
    HUNF ** p
    PROQ *** p
    SHWQ *** p
    SPIM ** p
    STOF ** p
    WATT ** p

Unseld, Westley. 1946-   .
United States. Basketball.
    CENT ** p/c
    GCPB *** p
    PBGR **
    WNQT ** p

Unser, Al. 1939-   . United
States. Automobile Racing.
    CIND *** p
    DOSW * p
    MARS ** p
    WGRD ** p

Unser, Bobby. 1934-   . United
States. Automobile Racing.
    CIND *** p
    DOSW * p
    MARS ** p
    SPKS *** p
    WGRD *** p

Unser, Delbert B. 1944-   .
United States. Baseball.
    SPSP ** p

Upshaw, Gene. 1945-   . United
States. Football.
    FCBL ** p

Valentine, Greg see Hammer,
The

Valenzuela, Fernando. 1960-   .
Mexico. Baseball.
    BASS * p/c

Valiant, Jimmy. Birthdate?
United States. Wrestling.
    WRES ** p

Van Brocklin, Norm. [b. Norman
Mack]. 1926- . United States.
Football.
    FCQB ** p
    GPQU ** p

Van Buren, Steve. 1920?- .
Honduras. Football.
    FRRB ** p
    GPRB ** p
    GRBF *** p
    GRUN ** p
    HUNF ** p

Vance, Dazzy. [b. Clarence
Arthur]. 1891-1961. United
States. Baseball.
    BFAM * i

Van Impe, Edward Charles.
1940- . Canada. Hockey.
    GDEF ** p/c
    UFTM *** p

van Wolvelaere, Patty. 1951?- .
United States. Track and Field.
    WSTF ** p

Vardon, Harry. 1870-1937.
Great Britain. Golf.
    GTGO *** p

Vare, Glenna Collett see Collett,
Glenna

Veeck, Bill. [b. William Louis].
1914-1986. United States.
Baseball [owner].
    CHCH **

Ventura, Jesse see Body, The

Venturi, Kenneth. 1931- .
United States. Golf.
    GIFC ****
    GOLF ***
    SHWQ ** p

Versalles, Zoilo. 1940- . Cuba.
Baseball.
    GLSF *** p

Vessels, Billy Dale. 1931- .
United States. Football.
    HATG **
    HEIS ** p

Vidmar, Peter. 1962?- . United
States. Gymnastics.
    MLRG * p

Vilas, Guillermo. 1952- .
Argentina. Tennis.
    WMOT ** p

Vingo, Carmine. 1929- . United
States? Boxing.
    BEYD **

Vinson-Owen, Maribel. 1911-
1961. United States. Ice Skating.
    AWIS * p
    HUNW * p

Viren, Lasse. 1949- . Finland.
Track and Field.
    MOSS *** p
    TGCH ** p

Von der Ahe, Chris. [b. Christian Frederick Wilhelm]. 1851-1913. West Germany. Baseball [owner].
  HUNB ** p

Von Erich, David. ?-1984. United States. Wrestling.
  WRES *

Von Erich, Kerry. Birthdate? United States. Wrestling.
  WRES * p

Von Erich, Kevin. Birthdate? United States. Wrestling.
  WRES *

Von Raschke, Baron. Birthdate? United States? Wrestling.
  WRE2 ** p

von Saltza, Chris. [b. Susan Christina]. 1944-   . United States. Swimming.
  AWIS ** p

Voss, J. C. 18____-   . Canada. Sailing.
  THSA ***

Vukovich, Bill. 1919-1955. United States. Automobile Racing.
  ARYL ** p
  CIND *** p
  GARD ** p
  GDGR **
  GMIN **

Vukovich, Billy. 1943?-   . United States. Automobile Racing.
  ARYL ** p
  KOMS ** p

Waddell, Rube. [b. George Edward]. 1876-1914. United States. Baseball.
  BZAN *** p
  HOFB ** p
  HUNB ** p

Wade, Virginia. 1945-   . South Africa. Tennis.
  CSPS ** p
  FWTP *** p
  QOTC ** p

Wagner, Honus. [b. John Peter]. 1874-1955. United States. Baseball.
  BATA ** p
  BFAM * i
  GISP ** i
  HOFB ** p
  HOHR ** p
  HUNB ** p
  SMAA ****
  TSBG ** p

Waitz, Grete Andersen. 1953-   . Norway. Track and Field.
  MARA * p
  SWTR *** p
  WCMA ** p

Wakely, Ernie. [b. Ernest Alfred]. 1940-   . Canada. Hockey.
  UFTM *** p

103

Walasiewicz, Stanislawa *see*
Walsh, Stella

Walcott, Jersey Joe. [b. Arnold
Raymond CREAM]. 1914- .
United States. Boxing.
    BHCF ** p
    HWCH * p
    POBS * p
    SFST ** p

Walk, Neal Eugene. 1948- .
United States. Basketball.
    ROOK ** p

Walker, Doak. [b. Ewell Doak
Jr]. 1927- . United States.
Football.
    HATG **
    HEIS ** p
    SHWQ ** p
    WHET ** p

Walker, Herschel. 1962- .
United States. Football.
    HATG **
    WHET ** p

Walker, Jimmy. 1944- . United
States. Basketball.
    SOPB *** p

Walker, John. 1951- . New
Zealand. Track and Field.
    TRMM ** p

Walker, Moses Fleetwood. 1857-
1924. United States. Baseball.
    POBS ** p

Walker, Wayne. 1936- . United
States. Football.
    GLBN *** p

Walker, Weldy Wilberforce.
1860-1937. United States.
Baseball.
    POBS *** p

Walker, Wesley Darcel. 1955- .
United States. Football.
    FSHR ** p
    NFLS * p/c

Wallace, Cookie. Birthdate?
United States. Boxing.
    BEYD **

Walls, Everson Collins. 1959- .
United States. Football.
    FDDB ** p

Walsh, Stella. [b. Stanislawa
WALASIEWICZ2]. 1911-1980.
Poland. Track and Field.
    AWIS ** p
    HUNW ** p

Walton, Bill. [b. William
Woodrow]. 1952- . United
States. Basketball.
    BHFL ** p
    CENT ** p/c
    CHCH **
    LONH *** p

Waltrip, Darrell. 1947- .
United States. Automobile
Racing.
    SCHA *** p

Wambsganss, Bill. [b. William
Adolph]. 1894- . United States.
Baseball.
  GOTT ** p

Waner, Lloyd James. 1906-
1982. United States. Baseball.
  BFAM * i
  HUNB ** p

Waner, Paul Glee. 1903-1965.
United States. Baseball.
  BFAM * i
  GOTT *** p
  HUNB ** p

Ward, Monte. [b. John
Montgomery]. 1860-1925.
United States. Baseball.
  PIBB ** p

Ward, Rodger. 1921- . United
States. Automobile Racing.
  CIND *** p
  GARD ** p
  SUPD *** p

Warfield, Paul D. 1942- .
United States. Football.
  GPCP *** p
  PFHT ** p
  RECS ** p, p/c
  SPRN *** p

Warmerdam, Cornelius. 1915- .
United States. Track and Field.
  GISP ** i

Warner, Pop. [b. Glenn Scobey].
1871-1954. United States.
Football.
  GIND ** p

HUNF ** p

Washington, Gene Alden.
1947- . United States. Football.
  CHMP ** i/c
  PFHT ** p

Waterfield, Bob. [b. Robert
Staton]. 1920- . United States.
Football.
  FCQB ** p
  HUNF ** p

Watson, John. 1946- . Ireland.
Automobile Racing.
  RACE ** p

Watson, Tom. 1949- . United
States. Golf.
  SSOG *** p

Weatherly, Little Joe. [b. Joseph
Herbert]. 1922-1964. United
States. Automobile Racing.
  GARD * p
  HSCR ** p

Weaver, Earl Sidney. 1930- .
United States. Baseball.
  BABM ** p
  BGMA *** p
  SGBM ** p
  TSBG ** p

Webb, Spud. [b. Anthony
Jerome]. 1963- . United States.
Basketball.
  YANF ** p

Weber, Dick. [b. Richard
Anthony]. 1929-   . United
States. Bowling.
    ASHT ** p

Webster, Mike. [b. Michael
Lewis]. 1952-   . United States.
Football.
    FCBL ** p

Weiskopf, Tom. [b. Thomas].
1942-   . United States. Golf.
    SSOG *** p

Weissmuller, Johnny. 1904-
1984. United States. Swimming.
    BEYD **
    SOTO **
    SPIM ** p
    WUND *** p

Weld, Tee. [b. Theresa]. [m.
Blanchard]. 1893-1978. United
States. Ice Skating.
    HUNW ** p

Wene, Sylvia. [m. Martin].
1928?-   . United States.
Bowling.
    AWIS **

West, Jerry. [b. Jerome Alan].
1938-   . United States.
Basketball.
    ASHT ** p
    BEYD **
    BSTG *** p
    CHMP ** i/c
    FPBS ** p
    GSTN *** p

Westphal, Paul. 1950-   . United
States. Basketball.
    BSHP ** p

White, Bill. [b. William D].
1934-   . United States.
Baseball.
    BPTH *** p

White, Charles Raymond.
1958-   . United States. Football.
    HATG *

White, Danny. 1952-   . United
States. Football.
    NFLS * p/c

White, Jo Jo. [b. Joseph]. 1946-
1986. United States. Basketball.
    ROOK ** p

White, Randy Lee. 1953-   .
United States. Football.
    FPPR ** p
    MSLB ** p, p/c
    NFLS * p/c
    SBWL ** p

White, Roy Hilton. 1943-   .
United States. Baseball.
    OTWU ** p
    WATT ** p

White, Stan. Birthdate? United
States. Football.
    MSLB ** p, p/c

White, Whizzer. [b. Byron
Raymond]. 1917-   . United
States. Football.
    HUNF ** p

White, Willye. 1939-   . United
States. Track and Field.
  GOLG ** p

Whitworth, Kathy. [b.
Kathrynne Ann]. 1939-   .
United States. Golf.
  FMAW *** p
  WOWW *** p

Widing, Juha Markku. 1947-   .
Finland. Hockey.
  HSSE **

Wightman, Hazel Hotchkiss *see*
Hotchkiss, Hazel

Wiley, Gene. Birthdate? United
States. Basketball.
  LONII ** p

Wilhelm, Hoyt. [b. James Hoyt].
1923-   . United States.
Baseball.
  HUNB ** p
  RBML ** p
  SPML *** p
  TSBG ** p

Wilkens, Lenny. [b. Leonard].
1937-   . United States.
Basketball.
  UHPB *** p

Wilkins, Alonzo. 1928?-1972.
United States. Basketball.
  GLTR ** p

Wilkins, Debbie. Birthdate?
United States. Motorcycle
Racing.
  WISM ** p

Wilkinson, Bud. [b. Charles
Burnham]. 1916-   . United
States. Football.
  SGFC ** p

Willard, Jess. 1881-1968.
United States. Boxing.
  HWCH * p
  POBS ** p
  SFST ** p

Willard, Ken. [b. Kenneth H].
1943-   . United States. Football.
  GRBF *** p
  SRBN ** p

Williams, Billy Leo. 1938-   .
United States. Baseball.
  UHML *** p

Williams, Buck. [b. Charles
Linwood]. 1960-   . United
States. Basketball.
  BAPP ** p

Williams, Dick. [b. Richard
Hirschfield]. 1928-   . United
States. Baseball.
  BABM ** p
  BGMA *** p

Williams, Joe. 1886-1946.
United States. Baseball.
  PIBB **

Williams, Ted. [also known as
The Kid]. [b. Theodore Samuel].
1918-   . United States.
Baseball.
  AHRK **
  BATA ** p
  BEYD **

BFAM * i
BGSL *** p
BHRH ** p
BIBA ***
BOBG ** p
CHAB **** p, i
GAML ***
GBST ** p
GCIS ** p
GISP ** i
GRLS ** p
HOFB ** p
HOHR *** p
HUNB ** p
PIBB *** p
RBML ** p
SMAA ****
SPIM ** p
TSBG ** p
WATT ** p
WWOS ** p

Wills, Helen. [m. Moody and
Roark]. 1905- . United States.
Tennis.
    AWIS ** p
    CTTC ** p
    CWSP *
    FWTP *** p
    GOLG ** p
    HUNW ** p
    QOTC ** p
    SPIM ** p
    TENN **
    WWOT ** p

Wills, Maury. [b. Maurice
Morning]. 1932- . United
States. Baseball.
    ASHT ** p
    GBST ** p
    WATT ** p

Wilson, Hack. [b. Lewis R.].
1900-1948. United States.
Baseball.
    BFAM * i

Wilson, Larry. [b. Lawrence
Frank]. 1938- . United States.
Football.
    ASHT ** p

Wilt the Stilt see Chamberlain,
Wilt

Windham, Barry. Birthdate?
United States. Wrestling.
    WRES ** p

Winfield, Dave. [b. David Mark].
1951- . United States.
Baseball.
    BAPH ** p
    BASS * p/c

Winslow, Kellen. 1957- .
United States. Football.
    NFLS * p/c

Witte, Luke. 1950- . United
States. Basketball.
    SUSS ** p

Wonderful, Mr. see Mr.
Wonderful

Wood, Smokey Joe. [b. Joseph].
1889-1985. United States.
Baseball.
    GOTT *** p

Wooden, John R. 1910- .
United States. Basketball.
    COAL ** p

Worsley, Gump. [b. Lorne].
1929-   . Canada. Hockey.
  FHPL *** p
  GGPH *** p
  MITN *** p

Worthington, Red. [b. Allan
Fulton]. 1929-   . United States.
Baseball.
  WATT ** p

Wottle, Dave. 1950-   . United
States. Track and Field.
  SOTO ** p

Wright, Harry. [b. William
Henry]. 1835-1895. Great
Britain. Baseball.
  PIBB ** p

Wright, Mickey. [b. Mary
Kathryn]. 1935-   . United
States. Golf.
  AWIS **
  HUNW * p
  WWOS ** p

Wright, Thelma. Birthdate?
Canada. Track and Field.
  WSTF ** p

Wyshner, Peter J. see Gray, Pete

Yankee Clipper see DiMaggio,
Joe

Yarborough, Cale. [b. William
Caleb]. 1939-   . United States.
Automobile Racing.
  DOSW * p
  GARD ** p
  HSCR *** p

Yarbrough, Lee Roy. 1938-   .
United States. Automobile
Racing.
  GARD ** p
  HSCR *** p

Yastrzemski, Carl Michael.
1939-   . United States.
Baseball.
  ASHT ** p
  CHMP ** p/c, i/c
  TSBG ** p

Yepremian, Garo. [b. Garabed
Sarkis]. 1944-   . Cyprus.
Football.
  FSTK ** p

Yost, Fielding Harris. 1871-
1946. United States. Football.
  SGFC ** p

Young, Candy. [b. Canzetta].
1962-   . United States. Track
and Field.
  SWTR *** p

Young, Cy. [b. Denton T.]. 1867-
1955. United States. Baseball.
  BFAM * i
  BLPC *** p
  GISP ** i
  HOFB ** p
  HUNB ** p

Young, Sheila. 1950-   . [m.
Ochowicz]. United States.
Bicycle Racing and Ice Skating.
  GOLG ** p
  MOSS *** p
  WOTI ** p

Young, Wilbur. 1949- . United
States. Football.
  SPSP ** p

Yount, Robin R. 1955- . United
States. Baseball.
  INFD ** p, p/c
  WUND *** p

Zaharias, Babe Didrikson *see*
Didrikson, Babe

Zale, Tony. [b. Anthony Florian
ZALESKI]. 1913- . United
States. Boxing.
  WATT ** p

Zatopek, Emil. 1922- .
Czechoslovakia. Track and Field.
  MARA **

TGCH *** p
WCMA ** p

Zayak, Elaine. 1966?- . United
States. Ice Skating.
  STOI ** p

Zbyszko, Larry. Birthdate?
United States. Wrestling.
  WRE2 ** p

Zorn, Jim. 1953- . United
States. Football.
  FWQB ** p

Zybina, Galina. Birthdate?
Union of Soviet Socialist
Republics. Track and Field.
  GOLG ** p

Part Two
Indexes

Index to Sports Figures by Sport

Airplane Racing

Joersz, Eldon, 50
Knight, Pete, 55
Morgan, George T., 70

Automobile Racing

Allison, Bobby, 4
Andretti, Mario, 5
Arfons, Art, 5
Arfons, Walt, 5
Arnold, Billy, 6
Ascari, Alberto, 6
Baker, Buck, 7
Baker, Buddy, 7
Beck, Gary, 9
Bettenhausen, Gary, 10
Bettenhausen, Merle, 10
Bettenhausen, Tony, 10
Bettenhausen, Tony Lee, 10
Brabham, Jack, 13
Brambilla, Vittorio, 14
Breedlove, Craig, 14
Bryan, Jimmy, 16
Campbell, Donald Malcolm, 17
Campbell, Malcolm, 17
Caracciola, Rudolf, 18
Carter, Duane, 18
Carter, Duane Jr., 18
Chiron, Louis Alexander, 20
Clark, Jim, 20
Cobb, John, 21
Cooper, Earl, 23
Depailler, Patrick, 27
DePalma, Ralph, 27
Donohue, Mark, 28
Easley, Sonny, 29
Eyston, George Edward, 30

Fangio, Juan Manuel, 31
Farina, Giuseppe, 31
Fittipaldi, Emerson, 32
Flock, Tim, 32
Follmer, George, 32
Foyt, A. J., 33
Gabelich, Gary, 35
Garlits, Don, 35
Ginther, Richie, 37
Glidden, Bob, 37
Golden, Maverick, 37
Gordon, Al, 38
Granatelli, Andy, 38
Gregg, Peter, 39
Gurney, Dan, 40
Guthrie, Janet, 41
Hall, Jim, 41
Harroun, Ray, 42
Hawley, Don, 43
Hawthorn, John Michael, 43
Heath, Allen, 43
Hill, Graham, 45
Hill, Philip Toll, 45
Holbert, Al, 46
Horn, Ted, 46
Hulme, Denis Clive, 48
Hunt, James Simon Wallis, 48
Hurtubise, Hercules, 48
Insolo, Jimmy, 48
Jarier, Jean-Pierre, 49
Jarrett, Ned Miller, 49
Johncock, Gordon, 50
Johnson, Junior, 50
Jones, Alan, 51
Jones, Parnelli, 51
Kenyon, Mel, 53
Laffite, Jacques, 56
Lauda, Niki, 57
Levegh, Pierre, 58

Lockhart, Frank, 59
Lombardi, Lella, 60
Lorenzen, Fred, 60
Lunger, Brett, 61
McCluskey, Roger, 62
McElreath, Jim, 63
McEwen, Mongoose, 63
McLaren, Bruce, 64
Mass, Jochen, 67
Mays, Rex, 68
Mears, Rick, 68
Mears, Roger, 68
Merzario, Arturo, 68
Meyer, Billy, 68
Meyer, Louis, 68
Miles, Ken, 69
Milton, Tommy, 69
Moss, Stirling Crauford, 71
Muldowney, Cha Cha, 71
Mulligan, Zookeeper, 71
Murphy, Jimmy, 72
Nuvolari, Tazio, 74
Oldfield, Barney, 75
O'Neil, Kitty Linn, 75
Ongais, Danny, 75
Pace, Carlos, 76
Parsons, Johnnie, 77
Parsons, Johnny, 77
Pearson, David, 77
Penske, Captain, 78
Peterson, Ronnie, 78
Petty, Lee, 79
Petty, Richard Lee, 79
Pollard, Art, 80
Posey, Sam, 80
Prudhomme, Snake, 81
Pryce, Tom, 81
Redman, Brian, 81
Regazzoni, Clay, 82
Reutemann, Carlos, 82
Revson, Peter Jeffrey, 82
Rickenbacker, Eddie, 83
Rindt, Karl-Jochen, 83
Roberts, Fireball, 83
Rose, Doug, 85
Rose, Mauri, 85
Sachs, Eddie, 87
Scheckter, Jody, 89
Shaw, Wilbur, 90
Shelby, Carroll, 90

Shuman, Ron, 91
Sneva, Tom, 93
Snively, Mike, 93
Stewart, Jackie, 95
Stuck, Hans Joachim, 95
Summers, Bob, 96
Surtees, John, 96
Tanner, Sammy, 96
Thompson, Dannie, 98
Thompson, Mickey, 98
Thomson, Johnny, 98
Triplett, Ernie, 100
Turner, Pops, 100
Unser, Al, 101
Unser, Bobby, 101
Vukovich, Bill, 103
Vukovich, Billy, 103
Waltrip, Darrell, 104
Ward, Rodger, 105
Watson, John, 105
Weatherly, Little Joe, 105
Yarborough, Cale, 109
Yarbrough, Lee Roy, 109

Baseball

Aaron, Hank, 3
Alexander, Pete, 3
Allen, Dick, 4
Almon, Bill, 4
Alou, Felipe Rojas, 4
Alston, Walter Emmons, 4
Anderson, Sparky, 4
Anson, Cap, 5
Aparicio, Luis Ernesto, 5
Appling, Luke, 5
Ashford, Emmett Littleton, 6
Austin, Jimmy, 6
Baines, Harold D., 7
Baker, Frank, 7
Bando, Sal, 7
Banks, Ernie, 7
Bearden, Gene, 8
Beckert, Glenn Alfred, 9
Belinsky, Bo, 9
Bell, Buddy, 9
Bench, Johnny Lee, 9
Bender, Charles Albert, 9
Berg, Morris, 10
Berra, Yogi, 10

Blue, Vida Rochelle, 12
Blyleven, Bert, 12
Boggs, Wade Anthony, 12
Bonds, Bobby Lee, 12
Bostock, Lyman Jr., 13
Bottomley, Jim, 13
Boyd, Oil Can, 13
Boyer, Clete, 13
Boyer, Ken, 13
Bresnahan, Duke, 14
Bressler, Rube, 14
Brett, George Howard, 14
Bridwell, Albert Henry, 14
Brock, Lou, 14
Brown, Mordecai Peter, 15
Browning, Pete, 16
Bunning, Jim, 16
Burdett, Lew, 16
Burgess, Smoky, 16
Burroughs, Jeff, 16
Campanella, Roy, 17
Campaneris, Bert, 17
Canseco, José, 17
Carew, Rod, 18
Carlton, Steve, 18
Carter, Gary Edmund, 18
Cartwright, Alexander J., 18
Cedeno, Cesar, 19
Cepeda, Perucho, 19
Chance, Frank Leroy, 19
Charboneau, Joe, 19
Chase, Hal, 20
Clarke, Fred, 21
Clemens, Roger William, 21
Clemente, Roberto Walker, 21
Cobb, Ty, 21
Cochrane, Mickey, 21-22
Colavito, Rocky, 22
Colbert, Nate, 22
Collins, Eddie, 22
Collins, Jimmy, 22
Comiskey, Charles Albert, 22
Concepcion, David Ismael, 22
Coveleski, Stanley Anthony, 23
Crawford, Wahoo Sam, 24
Cronin, Joe, 24
Cuellar, Mike, 25
Darling, Ron, 25
Davis, Eric, 25
Day, Pea Ridge, 26

Dean, Daffy, 26
Dean, Dizzy, 26
Delahanty, Ed, 26
Dickey, Bill, 27
DiMaggio, Joe, 28
Drabowsky, Moe, 28
Dressen, Charles Walter, 29
Drysdale, Don, 29
Durocher, Leo Ernest, 29
Ehmke, Howard John, 29
Essegian, Chuck, 30
Evers, John Joseph, 30
Fairly, Ron, 31
Feller, Bob, 31
Fidrych, Mark Steven, 31
Figueroa, Ed, 31
Fingers, Rollie, 31
Finley, Chuck, 31
Fisk, Carlton Ernest, 31
Flood, Curt, 32
Ford, Whitey, 32-33
Foster, George Arthur, 33
Foster, Rube, 33
Fowler, Bud, 33
Fox, Nellie, 33
Foxx, Jimmy, 33
Freehan, Bill, 34
Fregosi, Jim, 34
Frisch, Frank Francis, 34
Gaedel, Ed, 35
Gallagher, Alan, 35
Garvey, Steve, 35
Gehrig, Lou, 36
Gehringer, Charles Leonard, 36
Gibson, Bob, 36-37
Gibson, Joshua, 37
Gibson, Moon, 37
Gomez, Lefty, 37
Gooden, Dwight, 38
Goslin, Goose, 38
Gossage, Dick, 38
Grabarkewitz, Billy, 38
Grant, Frank Ulysses, 39
Gray, Peter, 39
Greenberg, Hank, 39
Grich, Bobby, 39
Groat, Dick, 40
Groh, Heinie, 40
Grote, Jerry, 40
Grove, Lefty, 40

Guerrero, Pedro, 40
Guglielmo, Angelo, 40
Guidry, Ron, 40
Guthrie, Bill, 40
Gutierrez, Coco, 41
Gwynn, Tony, 41
Harper, Tommy, 42
Harrelson, Bud, 42
Harrelson, Ken, 42
Harris, Bucky, 42
Hartnett, Gabby, 42
Hebner, Richard Joseph, 43
Henderson, Rickey, 44
Herman, Babe, 44
Hernandez, Keith, 44
Herr, Tom, 45
Herzog, Whitey, 45
Heyison, Marc, 45
Hiller, John Frederick, 45
Hodges, Gil, 45
Hooper, Harry Bartholomew, 46
Hornsby, Rajah, 46
Howard, Elston Gene, 46
Howard, Frank Oliver, 46
Hoy, Bill, 47
Hrabosky, Al, 47
Hubbell, King Carl, 47
Hubbs, Kenneth Douglass, 47
Huggins, Miller James, 47
Hundhammer, Paul, 48
Hunt, Ron, 48
Hunter, Catfish, 48
Irvin, Monte, 48
Jackson, Reggie, 49
Jenkins, Ferguson Arthur, 49
Jennings, Hugh Ambrose, 49
John, Tommy, 50
Johnson, Barney, 50
Johnstone, Jay, 51
Jones, Kangaroo, 51
Jones, Samuel Pond, 52
Kaline, Al, 52
Kamm, Willie, 52
Keeler, Wee Willie, 53
Kell, George Clyde, 53
Kelly, King, 53
Kemp, Steve, 53
Keough, Matt, 53
Killebrew, Harmon Clayton, 54
Kiner, Ralph McPherran, 54

Kingman, Dave, 55
Kitt, Howard, 55
Kittle, Ron, 55
Klem, Bill, 55
Koosman, Jerry, 55
Koufax, Sandy, 56
Lajoie, Larry, 56
Leach, Tommy, 58
Lee, Bill, 58
LeFlore, Ron, 58
Lemongello, Mark, 58
Lloyd, John Henry, 59
Lobert, Hans, 59
Lolich, Mickey, 60
Lombardi, Ernie, 60
Lopez, Al, 60
Lowenstein, John Lee, 61
Luciano, Ron, 61
Lurtsema, Bob, 61
Lyle, Sparky, 61
Lynn, Fred, 61
McCarthy, Joe, 62
McCarver, Tim, 62
McCovey, Stretch, 62
McDowell, Sam, 62
McGee, Willie, 63
McGinnity, Joe, 63
McGraw, Muggsy, 63
McGraw, Tug, 63
Mack, Connie, 63
McKechnie, Bill, 64
McLain, Denny, 64
McMullen, Ken, 64
Magerkurth, George Levi, 64
Maloney, Jim, 65
Mantle, Mickey Charles, 65
Maranville, Rabbit, 65
Marichal, Juan Antonio, 66
Maris, Roger Eugene, 66
Marquard, Rube, 66
Marshall, Mike, 66
Martin, Billy, 66
Martin, Pepper, 66
Mathews, Eddie, 67
Mathewson, Christy, 67
Matlack, Johnny, 67
Mattingly, Don, 67
Mayberry, John Claiborn, 67
Mays, Carl William, 67
Mays, Willie Howard, 68

Melton, Bill, 68
Meyers, Chief, 68
Minton, Greg, 69
Mize, John Robert, 69
Mizell, Vinegar Bend, 69
Morgan, Joe, 70
Mota, Manny, 71
Munson, Thurman Lee, 71
Murcer, Bobby Ray, 71
Murphy, Dale, 72
Murphy, John Joseph, 72
Murray, Eddie Clarence, 72
Murtaugh, Dan, 72
Musial, Stan, 72
Nettles, Graig, 73
Newsom, Bobo, 73
Niekro, Phil, 73
Nuxhall, Joe, 74
O'Doul, Lefty, 74
O'Farrell, Bob, 75
Oliva, Tony, 75
Oliver, Al, 75
Ott, Mel, 75
Paige, Satchel, 76
Palmer, Jim, 76
Parker, Dave, 77
Patkin, Max, 77
Perez, Tony, 78
Perry, Gaylord Jackson, 78
Petrocelli, Rico, 79
Phillips, Lefty, 79
Piersall, Jim, 79
Plank, Eddie, 80
Powell, Boog, 80
Puckett, Kirby, 81
Quisenberry, Dan, 81
Rader, Doug, 81
Reese, Pee Wee, 82
Reiser, Pete, 82
Rice, Jim, 82
Rickey, Branch, 83
Ripken, Cal, 83
Rizzuto, Phil, 83
Roberts, Robin Evan, 83
Robinson, Brooks Calbert, 84
Robinson, Frank, 84
Robinson, Jackie, 84
Robinson, Wilbert, 84
Rodriguez, Aurelio, 85
Rojas, Cookie, 85

Rose, Pete, 85
Roush, Edd J., 86
Rudi, Joe, 86
Ruth, Babe, 87
Ryan, Nolan, 87
Saberhagen, Bret William, 87
Sandberg, Ryne Dee, 88
Sanguillen, Manny, 88
Santo, Ron, 88
Schaefer, Germany, 89
Schmidt, Mike, 89
Schoendienst, Red, 89
Score, Herb, 89
Scott, George, 90
Seaver, Tom, 90
Simmons, Al, 91
Simmons, Ted Lyle, 91
Sisler, George Harold, 92
Skowron, Bill, 92
Smith, Ozzie, 92
Snider, Duke, 93
Snodgrass, Snow, 93
Sockalexis, Louis, 93
Spahn, Warren Edward, 93
Spalding, A. G., 93
Speaker, Spoke, 93
Stanhouse, Don, 94
Stargell, Willie, 94
Stengel, Casey, 94-95
Stone, Steve, 95
Stoneham, Horace, 95
Strawberry, Darryl Eugene, 95
Sunday, Billy, 96
Sutter, Bruce, 96
Tekulve, Ken, 97
Tenace, Gene, 97
Terry, Bill, 97
Thomas, Gorman, 98
Thomson, Bobby, 98
Throneberry, Marvin Eugene, 98
Tiant, Luis Clemente, 98
Tinker, Joe, 99
Toporcer, Specs, 99
Torre, Joe, 99
Traynor, Pie, 99
Turley, Bob, 100
Uecker, Bob, 101
Unser, Delbert B., 101
Valenzuela, Fernando, 101
Vance, Dazzy, 102

117

Veeck, Bill, 102
Versalles, Zoilo, 102
Von der Ahe, Chris, 103
Waddell, Rube, 103
Wagner, Honus, 103
Walker, Moses Fleetwood, 104
Walker, Weldy Wilberforce, 104
Wambsganss, Bill, 105
Waner, Lloyd James, 105
Waner, Paul Glee, 105
Ward, Monte, 105
Weaver, Earl Sidney, 105
White, Bill, 106
White, Roy Hilton, 106
Wilhelm, Hoyt, 107
Williams, Billy Leo, 107
Williams, Dick, 107
Williams, Joe, 107
Williams, Ted, 107-108
Wills, Maury, 108
Wilson, Hack, 108
Winfield, Dave, 108
Wood, Smokey Joe, 108
Worthington, Red, 109
Wright, Harry, 109
Yastrzemski, Carl Michael, 109
Young, Cy, 109
Yount, Robin R., 110

Basketball

Abdul-Jabbar, Kareem, 3
Archibald, Nate, 5
Arizin, Paul, 5
Attles, Alvin, 6
Auerbach, Red, 6
Barry, Rick, 7
Baylor, Ed, 8
Bellamy, Walt, 9
Belmont, Joe, 9
Bing, Dave, 11
Bird, Larry, 11
Birdsong, Otis, 11
Blazejowski, Carol, 12
Bradley, Bill, 13
Bridgeman, Junior, 14
Brown, Roger, 15
Brown, Walter, 16
Buckner, Quinn, 16
Cartwright, Bill, 18

Chamberlain, Wilt, 19
Collins, Doug, 22
Costello, Larry, 23
Cousy, Bob, 23
Cowens, David William, 24
Cummings, Terry, 25
Cunningham, Billy, 25
Daniels, Mel, 25
Dantley, Adrian, 25
Davis, Johnny, 26
DeBusschere, Dave, 26
Erving, Julius, 30
Fitch, Bill, 31
Ford, Phil, 32
Frazier, Clyde, 34
Free, World B., 34
Fulks, Joe, 34
Gervin, George, 36
Gilmore, Artis, 37
Greer, Hal, 39
Havlicek, John, 42-43
Hawkins, Connie, 43
Hayes, Elvin, 43
Haywood, Spencer, 43
Heinsohn, Tom, 44
Holman, Nathan, 46
Holzman, Red, 46
Hudson, Lou, 47
Issel, Dan, 49
Johnson, Gus, 50
Johnson, Magic, 51
Johnson, Marques, 51
Jones, Bobby, 51
Jones, K. C., 52
Jones, Sam, 52
Kerr, John, 54
King, Bernie, 54
King, Dolly, 54
Lanier, Bob, 57
Layne, Floyd, 58
Loscutoff, Jim, 60
Love, Bob, 60
Lovellette, Clyde, 60
Lucas, Jerry, 61
Lucas, John, 61
Lucas, Maurice, 61
McAdoo, Bob, 61-62
Macauley, Ed, 62
McDaniels, Jim, 62
McGill, Billy, 63

McGinnis, George, 63
McKoy, Wayne, 64
Malone, Moses, 65
Maravich, Peter Press, 65
Martin, Dugie, 66
Martin, LaRue, 66
Mikan, George Lawrence, 69
Monroe, Earl, 70
Motta, Dick, 71
Mullin, Mo, 71
Murphy, Cal, 71
Nater, Swen, 73
Newlin, Mike, 73
Nixon, Norm Charles, 74
Paultz, Billy, 77
Petrie, Geoff, 78
Pettit, Bob, 79
Porter, Kevin, 80
Ramsey, Frank, 81
Reed, Willis, 81
Rivers, David, 83
Robertson, Oscar Palmer, 83
Robinson, David Maurice, 84
Roundfield, Dan, 86
Ruland, Jeff, 87
Russell, Bill, 87
Russell, Cazzie, 87
Sanders, Satch, 88
Schaus, Frederick, 89
Schayes, Dolph, 89
Scott, Charlie, 89
Seikaly, Rony, 90
Shank, Theresa, 90
Sharman, Bill, 90
Sikma, Jack, 91
Silas, James, 91
Sloan, Jerry, 92
Smith, Elmore, 92
Thompson, David, 98
Thurmond, Nate, 98
Unseld, Westley, 101
Walk, Neal Eugene, 104
Walker, Jimmy, 104
Walton, Bill, 104
Webb, Spud, 105
West, Jerry, 106
Westphal, Paul, 106
White, Jo Jo, 106
Wiley, Gene, 107
Wilkens, Lenny, 107

Wilkins, Alonzo, 107
Williams, Buck, 107
Witte, Luke, 108
Wooden, John R., 108

Bicycle Racing

Heiden, Eric, 44
Meiffret, José, 68
Young, Sheila, 109

Boat Racing

Campbell, Donald Malcolm, 17
Taylor, Lee, 97

Bowling

Carter, Don, 18
Ladewig, Marion, 56
McCutcheon, Floretta, 62
Soutar, Judy Cook, 93
Sperber, Paula, 93
Weber, Dick, 106
Wene, Sylvia, 106

Boxing

Ali, Muhammad, 3
Armstrong, Henry, 6
Baer, Max, 6
Berlenbach, Paul, 10
Braddock, James J., 13
Brown, Panama Al, 15
Burns, Tommy, 16
Carnera, Primo, 18
Cerdan, Marcel Jr., 19
Charles, Ezzard B., 19
Corbett, Gentleman Jim, 23
Dempsey, Jack, 27
Dixon, George, 28
Fitzsimmons, Robert, 32
Flowers, Tiger, 32
Ford, George, 32
Frazier, Joe, 34
Gans, Joe, 35
Graziano, Rocky, 39
Griffith, Emile Alphonse, 40
Hart, Marvin, 42
Jackson, Peter, 49

Jeffries, James Jackson, 49
Johansson, Ingemar, 50
Johnson, Jack, 50
Kabakoff, Harry, 52
LaMotta, Jake, 57
Langford, Sam, 57
Liston, Sonny, 59
Louis, Joe, 60
Marciano, Rocky, 65-66
Molineaux, Tom, 70
Nash, Charlie, 72
Nelson, Battling, 73
Norton, Ken, 74
Ortega, Gaspar, 75
Patterson, Floyd, 77
Pep, Willie, 78
Robinson, Sugar Ray, 84
Ross, Barney, 86
Saddler, Sandy, 87
Sardinias, Eligio, 88
Schmeling, Max, 89
Sharkey, Jack, 90
Siki, Battling, 91
Sullivan, John Lawrence, 95
Tunney, Gene, 100
Tyson, Mike, 100
Vingo, Carmine, 102
Walcott, Jersey Joe, 104
Wallace, Cookie, 104
Willard, Jess, 107
Zale, Tony, 110

Equestrian Sports
  see **Horseback Riding, Horse Racing, Horse Training, Polo**

Field Hockey

Applebee, Constance, 5

Football

Abramowicz, Danny, 3
Allen, George, 4
Allen, Marcus, 4
Alworth, Lance, 4
Ameche, Alan, 4
Anderson, Donny, 4
Anderson, Ken, 4
Baker, Bubba, 7
Baker, Terry Wayne, 7
Banks, Chip, 7
Barney, Lem, 7
Bass, Dick, 8
Battles, Clifford Franklin, 8
Baugh, Sammy, 8
Baughan, Maxie, 8
Baumhower, Bob, 8
Beban, Gary Joseph, 8
Bednarik, Chuck, 9
Bellino, Joe, 9
Benirschke, Rolf Joachim, 9
Bergey, Bill L., 10
Berry, Ray, 10
Bertelli, Angelo, 10
Berwanger, Jay, 10
Bierman, Bernie, 11
Biletnikoff, Fred
Bingaman, Lester, 11
Blair, Matt, 11
Blanchard, Doc, 12
Blanda, George F., 12
Bleier, Rocky, 12
Blood, Johnny, 12
Blount, Melvin, 12
Bradley, Bill, 13
Bradshaw, Terry Paxton, 14
Brazile, Bob, 14
Brickley, Charley, 14
Brockington, John, 14
Brodie, John, 15
Brown, Bill, 15
Brown, Bob, 15
Brown, Fred, 15
Brown, Jim, 15
Brown, Larry, 15
Brown, Paul, 15
Brown, Roger, 15
Bryant, Bear, 16
Buoniconti, Nick, 16
Butkus, Dick, 17
Butz, Dave, 17
Camp, Walter Chauncey, 17
Campbell, Earl Christian, 17
Cannon, Billy, 18
Carmichael, Harold, 18
Carr, Fred, 18
Casper, Dave, 19
Cassady, Hopalong, 19
Chamberlin, Guy, 19

Chester, Ray, 20
Clark, Dutch, 20
Clark, Dwight, 20
Collins, Gary, 22
Conerly, Charley, 22
Cook, Greg, 23
Cousineau, Tom, 23
Cox, Fred, 24
Cromwell, Nolan Neil, 24
Crow, John David, 24
Crowely, Jim, 24
Csonka, Larry, 24-25
Curtis, Isaac, 25
Curtis, Mike, 25
Davis, Allen, 25
Davis, Ernie, 25
Davis, Junior, 26
Dawkins, Pete, 26
Dawson, Len, 26
Dean, Fred, 26
DeLamielleure, Joe, 27
Dempsey, Tom, 27
Devaney, Bob, 27
Dickerson, Eric, 27
Dierdorf, Dan, 28
Dixon, Hewritt, 28
Dorsett, Tony, 28
Dudley, Bill, 29
Duncan, Jim, 29
Eller, Carl Lee, 30
Ellison, Willie, 30
Farr, Mel, 31
Federspiel, Joe, 31
Fencik, Gary, 31
Flutie, Doug, 32
Foreman, Chuck, 33
Fortmann, Danny, 33
Fouts, Dan, 33
Francis, Russell Ross, 33
Frank, Clinton Edward, 33
Franklin, Tony, 33
Friedman, Ben, 34
Fuqua, Frenchy, 35
Gabriel, Roman, 35
Garrett, Mike, 35
Giammona, Louie, 36
Gilchrist, Cookie, 37
Gilliam, John Rally, 37
Gipp, George, 37
Gogolak, Pete, 37

Gradisher, Randy, 38
Graham, Otto Everett Jr., 38
Grange, Red, 38-39
Granger, Hoyle, 39
Grant, Bud, 39
Gray, Leon, 39
Greene, Joe, 39
Grier, Rosey, 39
Griese, Bob, 40
Griffin, Archie Mason, 40
Groza, Louis Roy, 40
Guy, Ray, 41
Guyon, Joseph Napoleon, 41
Halas, George, 41
Ham, Jack Raphael, 41
Hannah, John Allen, 41
Harmon, Tom, 42
Harris, Franco, 42
Hart, Leon Joseph, 42
Hayes, Lester, 43
Hayes, Bob, 43
Hayes, Woody, 43
Haymond, Alvin Henry, 43
Haynes, Abner, 43
Haynes, Mike, 43
Heffelfinger, Pudge, 44
Hein, Melvin John, 44
Heisman, John William, 44
Hendricks, Ted, 44
Henry, Pete, 44
Herrera, Efren, 45
Heston, Willie, 45
Hill, Calvin, 45
Hinkey, Frank, 45
Hinkle, Clarke, 45
Hirsch, Crazylegs, 45
Hornung, Paul Vernon, 46
Horvath, Les, 46
Houston, Ken, 46
Howley, Chuck, 47
Huarte, John, 47
Hubbard, Cal, 47
Hutson, Don, 48
Janowicz, Vic, 49
Jefferson, John Larry, 49
Johnson, Big Hands, 50
Johnson, Bob, 50
Johnson, Charley, 50
Johnson, John Henry, 50
Johnson, Pete, 51

Johnson, Ron, 51
Jones, Bert, 51
Jones, Deacon, 51
Jordan, Lee Roy, 52
Jurgensen, Sonny, 52
Kapp, Joe, 52
Kazmaier, Dick, 53
Kelley, Larry, 53
Kelly, Leroy, 53
Kemp, Ray, 53
Kiesling, Walter A., 54
Kiick, Jim, 54
Kinnick, Nile Jr., 55
Klecko, Joe, 55
Klosterman, Don, 55
Kramer, Jerry, 56
Kramer, Ron, 56
Kunz, George, 56
Kwalick, Ted, 56
Ladd, Ernest, 56
Lambeau, Curly, 57
Lambert, Jack, 57
Lamonica, Daryle Pat, 57
Lancaster, Ron, 57
Landry, Greg, 57
Landry, Tom, 57
Lane, MacArthur, 57
Langer, Jim, 57
Lanier, Willie Edward, 57
Largent, Steve M., 57
Lattner, John Joseph, 57
Layden, Elmer F., 58
Layne, Bobby, 58
Leahy, Frank, 58
LeBaron, Edward W., 58
LeClair, Jim, 58
Lemm, Wally, 58
Lillard, Joe, 59
Lilly, Bob, 59
Lipscomb, Gene, 59
Little, Floyd Douglas, 59
Little, Larry C., 59
Lofton, James David, 59
Lombardi, Vince, 60
Lott, Ronnie, 60
Luckman, Sidney, 61
Lujack, John C., 61
Lyman, Link, 61
McAfee, George Anderson, 62
McDonald, Henry, 62

McDonald, Tommy, 62
McElhenny, Hugh, 62
McKay, John Harvey, 64
Mackey, John, 64
Manning, Archie, 65
Marcol, Chester, 66
Marshall, Jim, 66
Martin, Harvey, 66
Matson, Ollie, 67
Maynard, Don, 67
Meggyesy, Dave, 68
Miller, Don, 69
Mitchell, Bobby, 69
Montana, Joe, 70
Montgomery, Wilbert, 70
Moore, Lenny, 70
Morris, Mercury, 70
Morton, Craig L., 71
Motley, Marion, 71
Mount Pleasant, Frank, 71
Munoz, Anthony, 71
Nagurski, Bronko, 72
Namath, Joe, 72
Nance, Jim, 72
Nelsen, Bill, 73
Nevers, Ernie, 73
Newsome, Ozzie, 73
Niland, John Hugh, 73
Nitschke, Ray, 74
Nobis, Tommy, 74
Noll, Chuck, 74
O'Brien, Davey, 74
O'Dea, Patrick John, 74
Odoms, Riley, 74
Olsen, Merlin, 75
Owens, Steve, 76
Page, Al, 76
Parker, Jim, 77
Paterno, Joe, 77
Payton, Sweetness, 77
Pearson, Drew, 77
Peoples, Woody, 78
Perkins, Don, 78
Perry, Joe, 78
Perry, William, 78
Plunkett, Jim, 80
Plunkett, Sherman, 80
Pollard, Fritz, 80
Pont, John, 80
Post, Dick, 80

Powell, Marvin, 80
Prothro, Tommy, 80
Pruitt, Greg, 81
Rashad, Ahmad, 81
Reid, Mike, 82
Rentzel, Lance, 82
Riggins, John, 83
Robertson, Isiah, 83
Robeson, Paul LeRoy, 84
Robinson, Dave, 84
Robinson, Paul, 84
Robinson, Sugar Ray, 84
Rockne, Knute Kenneth, 85
Rodgers, Johnny, 85
Rogers, George Washington Jr., 85
Rossovich, Tim, 86
Roth, Joe, 86
Royal, Darrell K., 86
Rozelle, Pete, 86
Rozier, Mike, 86
Ruffin, Nate, 86
Russell, Andy, 87
Sanders, Charles A., 88
Santana, Tito, 88
Sauer, George H. Jr., 88
Sayers, Gale Eugene, 89
Scott, Jake, 90
Selmon, Lee Roy, 90
Shula, Don, 91
Siemon, Jeff, 91
Simpson, O. J., 91
Sims, Billy, 91
Sinkwich, Frank, 91
Smith, Bruce, 92
Smith, Bubba, 92
Snell, Matt, 93
Spurrier, Steve, 93
Stabler, Ken Michael, 94
Stagg, Amos Alonzo, 94
Stallworth, John, 94
Starr, Bart, 94
Staubach, Roger, 94
Stenerud, Jan, 94
Still, Art, 95
Stingley, Darryl, 95
Strong, Ken, 95
Stuhldreher, Harry, 95
Sullivan, Pat, 95
Swann, Lynn Curtis, 96
Tarkenton, Fran, 96

Tatum, Jack, 96
Taylor, Bruce Lawrence, 97
Taylor, Charles R., 97
Taylor, Jim, 97
Taylor, Larry, 97
Taylor, Otis, 97
Testaverde, Vinny, 97
Theismann, Joe, 97
Thomas, Duane, 97
Thomas, Pat Calvin, 98
Thorpe, Jim, 98
Tittle, Y. A., 99
Trafton, George, 99
Trippi, Charles Louis, 100
Tucker, Bob, 100
Tunnell, Emlen, 100
Turner, Bulldog, 100
Unitas, Johnny, 101
Unseld, Westley, 101
Upshaw, Gene, 101
Van Brocklin, Norm, 102
Van Buren, Steve, 102
Vessels, Billy Dale, 102
Walker, Doak, 104
Walker, Herschel, 104
Walker, Wayne, 104
Walker, Wesley Darcel, 104
Walls, Everson Collins, 104
Warfield, Paul D., 105
Warner, Pop, 105
Washington, Gene Alden, 105
Waterfield, Bob, 105
Webster, Mike, 106
White, Charles Raymond, 106
White, Danny, 106
White, Randy Lee, 106
White, Stan, 106
White, Whizzer, 106
Wilkinson, Bud, 107
Willard, Ken, 107
Wilson, Larry, 108
Winslow, Kellen, 108
Yepremian, Garo, 109
Yost, Fielding Harris, 109
Young, Wilbur, 110
Zorn, Jim, 110

Golf

Baugh, Laura Zonetta, 8

INDEX TO SPORTS FIGURES

Beard, Frank, 8
Berg, Patricia Jane, 10
Boswell, Charley, 13
Brown, Pete Earlie, 15
Casper, Billy, 19
Collett, Glenna, 22
Cotton, Henry, 23
Didrikson, Babe, 27-28
Floyd, Raymond, 32
Geiberger, Allen, 36
Gibson, Althea, 36
Hagen, Walter, 41
Hogan, Ben, 45-46
Irwin, Hale, 49
Jones, Bobby, 51
Joyce, Joan, 51
Lopez, Nancy, 60
Mann, Carol, 65
Miller, Johnny, 69
Nicklaus, Jack William, 73
Ouimet, Francis, 75
Palmer, Arnold Daniel, 76
Player, Gary, 80
Rankin, Judy, 81
Rodriguez, Chi-Chi, 85
Sarazon, Gene, 88
Snead, Sam, 92
Thomson, Peter, 98
Trevino, Lee Buck, 100
Vardon, Harry, 102
Venturi, Ken, 102
Watson, Tom, 105
Weiskopf, Tom, 106
Whitworth, Kathy, 107
Wright, Mickey, 109

Gymnastics

Andrianov, Nikolai, 5
Comaneci, Nadia, 22
Conner, Bart, 22
Daggett, Tim, 25
Gaylord, Mitch, 36
Gushiken, Koji, 40
Johnson, Kathy, 41
Kim, Nelli, 54
Korbut, Olga, 55
McNamara, Julianne, 64
Ning, Li, 74
Phillips, Kristie, 79

Retton, Mary Lou, 82
Rigby, Cathy, 83
Szabo, Ekaterina, 96
Tsukahara, Mitsuo, 100
Vidmar, Peter, 102

Hockey

Apps, Syl, 5
Barkley, Doug, 7
Bathgate, Andy, 8
Beliveau, Jean Marc, 9
Berenson, Red, 10
Binkley, Les, 11
Blair, Wren, 11
Blake, Toe, 12
Bossy, Michael, 13
Bower, John William, 13
Broda, Turk, 14
Brodeur, Richard, 15
Cheevers, Gerry, 20
Ciccarelli, Dino, 20
Clarke, Bobby, 20
Cournoyer, Yvan Serge, 23
Craig, Jim, 24
Crozier, Roger Allan, 24
Cushman, Wayne, 25
Delvecchio, Fats, 27
Dionne, Marcel, 28
Dryden, Ken, 29
Durnan, Bill, 29
Esposito, Phil, 30
Esposito, Tony, 30
Ferguson, John Bowie, 31
Fleming, Reggie, 32
Geoffrion, Boom Boom, 36
Giacomin, Edward, 36
Gilbert, Gilles, 37
Gilbert, Rod, 37
Goldsworthy, Bill, 37
Green, Ted, 39
Gretsky, Wayne, 39
Hall, Glenn Henry, 41
Harper, Terry, 42
Harvey, Doug, 42
Henderson, Paul Garnet, 44
Howe, Gordie, 47
Howe, Mark Steven, 47
Hull, Bobby, 47-48
Hull, Dennis William, 48

Imlach, Punch, 48
Johnston, Eddie, 51
Kelly, Red, 53
Keon, Dave, 53
Lafleur, Guy Damien, 56
Leach, Reggie, 58
Lindsay, Ted, 59
Liut, Mike, 59
Magnuson, Keith Arien, 64
Mahovlich, Frank, 64
Martin, Rick, 66
Mikita, Stanley, 69
Moog, Andy, 70
Morenz, Howie, 70
Neilson, Jim, 73
Orr, Bobby, 75
Palmateer, Mike, 76
Parent, Bernie, 76
Park, Brad, 76
Patrick, Lester, 77
Peeters, Pete, 78
Perreault, Gil, 78
Pilote, Pierre Paul, 79
Plante, Jacques, 80
Potvin, Denis Charles, 80
Ratelle, Jean, 81
Redmond, Mickey, 81
Resch, Chico, 82
Richard, Henri, 82
Richard, Rocket, 82
Sanderson, Turk, 88
Sawchuk, Terry, 88-89
Schmidt, Milton Conrad, 89
Schultz, Dave, 89
Shore, Edward William, 91
Sittler, Darryl Glen, 92
Smith, Billy, 92
Smythe, Conn Stafford, 92
Stasiuk, Vic, 94
Stastny, Peter, 94
Tallon, Dale, 96
Tkaczuk, Walter Robert, 99
Tremblay, J. C., 99
Tretiak, Vladislav, 99
Trottier, Bryan, 100
Ullman, Norman Victor, 101
Unger, Garry Douglas, 101
Van Impe, Edward Charles, 102
Wakely, Ernie, 103
Widing, Juha Markku, 107

Worsley, Gump, 109

Horseback Riding

Gurney, Hilda, 40
Sears, Eleo, 90

Horse Racing

Arcaro, Eddie, 5
Bacon, Mary, 6
Boudrot, Denise, 13
Cauthen, Steve, 19
Crump, Diane, 24
Hartack, Bill, 42
Kusner, Kathy, 56
Lvesque, Jean-Louis, 59
McCreary, Conn, 62
McEvoy, Michele, 63
Murphy, Isaac, 72
Rubin, Barbara Jo, 86
Shoemaker, Willie, 90
Smith, Robyn Caroline, 92
Turcotte, Ron, 100

Horse Training

Crabtree, Helen, 24

Ice Skating

Albright, Tenley Emma, 3
Allen, Lisa-Marie, 4
Babilonia, Tai Reina, 6
Beauchamp, Bobby, 8
Blumberg, Judy, 12
Button, Dick, 17
Chin, Tiffany, 20
Cramer, Scott, 24
Curry, John, 25
DeLeeuw, Dianne, 27
Fleming, Peggy Gale, 32
Fratianne, Linda Sue, 34
Gardner, Randy, 35
Hamill, Dorothy, 41
Hamilton, Scott, 41
Heiden, Beth, 44
Heiden, Eric, 44
Heiss, Carol, 44
Henie, Sonja, 44

Henning, Anne, 44
Lynn, Janet, 61
Magnussen, Karen, 64
Rodnina, Irina, 85
Santee, David, 88
Santee, James, 88
Seibert, Michael, 90
Shelley, Ken, 90
Smith, Stacy, 92
Starbuck, Jo Jo, 94
Summers, John, 96
Thomas, Debi, 97
Tickner, Charles, 98
Vinson-Owen, Maribel, 102
Weld, Tee, 106
Young, Sheila, 109
Zayak, Elaine, 110

Motorcycle Racing

Beck, Trudy, 9
Cox, Diane, 24
Fuller, Peggy, 34
Hawley, Don, 43
Karsmakers, Pierre, 52
Kirk, Tammy Jo, 55
Knievel, Evel, 55
O'Neil, Kitty Linn, 75
Patrick, Mike, 77
Payne, Nancy, 77
Rayborn, Calvin, 81
Resweber, Carroll, 82
Stenersen, Johanna, 94
Turton, Janene, 100
Wilkins, Debbie, 107

Mountain Climbing

Peck, Annie Smith, 78

Polo

Jones, Sue Sally, 52

Pool

Mizerak, Steve, 70

Rodeo

Brorsen, Metha, 15
Bussey, Shelia, 16
Fuchs, Becky, 34
Johnson, Dammy Williams, 50
Johnson, Trudy, 51
Pirtle, Sue, 79
Prudom, Benjie Bell, 81
Thurman, Sammy Fancher, 98

Rowing

Spock, Benjamin, 93

Sailing

Blackburn, Howard, 11
Blyth, Chay, 12
Caldwell, John, 17
Chichester, Francis, 20
Crowhurst, Donald, 24
Davison, Ann, 26
Gerbault, Alain, 36
Graham, Robin Lee, 38
Guzzwell, John, 41
McGregor, Rob Roy, 63
Pidgeon, Harry, 79
Rose, Alec, 85
Slocum, Joshua, 92
Voss, J.C., 103

Scuba Diving

Clark, Eugenie, 20
Earle, Sylvia, 29
Garner, Kati, 35
Parry, Zale, 77
Taylor, Valerie, 97

Skiing

Chaffee, Suzy, 19
Cochran, Barbara Ann, 21
Cochran, Linda, 21
Cochran, Marilyn, 21
Cochran, Mickey, 21
Fraser, Gretchen Kunigk, 34
Fuller, Genia, 34
Greene, Nancy, 39

Hlavaty, Jana, 45
Killy, Jean-Claude, 54
Kinmont, Jill, 55
Koch, Bill, 55
McKinney, Steve, 64
Mead, Andy, 68
Moser-Proell, Annemarie, 71
Nelson, Cindy, 73
Pitou, Penny, 79
Saudan, Sylvain, 88

Soccer

Beckenbauer, Franz, 9
Chinaglia, Giorgio, 20
Cruyff, Johan C., 24
McAlister, Jim, 62
Messing, Shep, 68
Pelé, 78
Rote, Kyle Jr., 86
Roth, Werner, 86
Trost, Al, 100

Softball

Joyce, Joan, 52

Sports Announcing

Cosell, Howard Cohen, 23

Swimming

Babashoff, Shirley, 6
Bartz, Jennifer, 8
Belote, Melissa Louise, 9
Berg, Sharon, 10
Chadwick, Florence May, 19
Curtis, Ann, 25
De Varona, Donna, 27
Ederle, Trudy, 29
Ender, Kornelia, 30
Fraser, Dawn, 34
Genesko, Lynn, 36
Gould, Shane Elizabeth, 38
Heddy, Kathy, 43
Johnson, Gail, 50
King, Micki, 54-55
Lee, Sammy, 58
Loock, Christine, 60

McCormick, Patty, 62
MacInnis, Nina, 63
Meyer, Debbie, 68
Nyad, Diana, 74
Schollander, Don, 89
Spitz, Mark Andrew, 93
Von Saltza, Chris, 103
Weissmuller, Johnny, 106

Tennis

Ashe, Arthur Robert A., 6
Austin, Tracy, 6
Becker, Boris, 9
Bjurstedt, Molla, 11
Borg, Bjorn, 13
Borotra, Jean, 13
Brugnon, Jacques, 16
Budge, Don, 16
Casals, Rosemary, 18
Cochet, Henri, 21
Connolly, Maureen, 22
Connors, Jimmy, 23
Court, Margaret Smith, 23
Evert, Chris, 30
Gibson, Althea, 36
Gonzales, Pancho, 38
Goolagong, Evonne, 38
Hoad, Lewis, 45
Hotchkiss, Hazel, 46
Jacobs, Helen Hull, 49
King, Billie Jean Moffitt, 54
Kramer, Jack, 56
Lacoste, Ren, 56
Laver, Rod, 58
Lenglen, Suzanne, 58
McEnroe, John, 63
Marble, Alice, 65
Nastase, Ilie, 73
Navratilova, Martina, 73
Perry, Fred, 78
Riggs, Bobby, 83
Rosewall, Ken, 85
Talbert, Billy, 96
Tilden, Bill, 99
Vilas, Guillermo, 102
Wade, Virginia, 103
Wills, Helen, 108

127

Track and Field

Ashford, Evelyn, 6
Balas, Iolanda, 7
Bannister, Roger Gilbert, 7
Barron, Ben, 7
Barron, Gayle, 7
Bayi, Filbert, 8
Beamon, Bob, 8
Benoit, Joan, 10
Bikila, Abebe, 11
Bingay, Roberta Gibb, 11
Bjorkland, Garry, 11
Blankers-Koen, Fanny, 12
Brumel, Valeri, 16
Campbell, Robin Theresa, 17
Carlos, John, 18
Carvajal, Felix, 18
Cheng, Chi, 20
Cierpinski, Waldemar, 20
Coe, Sebastian, 22
Cooksey, Marty, 23
Cunningham, Glenn, 25
Cuthbert, Betty, 25
Davis, Glenn, 26
Decker, Mary, 26
DeMar, Clarence H., 27
Didrikson, Babe, 27-28
Dillard, Harrison, 28
Drayton, Jerome, 29
Drechsler, Heike Daute, 29
Elliott, Herbert James, 30
Fikotova, Olga, 31
Frederick, Jane, 34
Fuchs, Ruth, 34
Hart, Eddie, 42
Hayes, Bob, 43
Hayes, Johnny, 43
Huntley, Joni, 48
Jackson, Nell, 49
Jenner, Bruce, 49
Johnson, Rafer Lewis, 51
Juantorena, Alberto, 52
Kazankina, Tatyana, 53
Keino, Kip, 53
Kelley, John Adelbert, 53
Kelley, John J., 53
Koch, Marita, 55
Kolehmainen, Hannes, 55
Larrieu, Francie, 57

Lewis, Carl, 59
Longboat, Tom, 60
Loues, Spyridon, 60
Manning, Madeline, 65
Mathias, Bob, 67
Matson, Randy, 67
Matthews, Vincent Edward, 67
Mauermayer, Gisela, 67
Miller, Kathy, 69
Mills, Billy, 69
Morcom, Boo, 70
Moses, Edwin, 71
Nurmi, Paavo Johannes, 74
O'Brien, Parry, 74
Oerter, Al, 75
Ovett, Steve, 76
Owens, Jesse, 76
Pheidippides, 79
Pietri, Dorando, 79
Rodgers, Bill, 85
Rosendahl, Heidemarie, 85
Rudolph, Wilma, 86
Ryun, Jim, 87
Salazar, Alberto, 88
Saneyev, Viktor, 88
Schmidt, Kathy, 89
Shea, Julie, 90
Shorter, Frank, 91
Slack, Mike, 92
Snell, Peter, 93
Stecher, Renate Meissner, 94
Strickland, Shirley, 95
Switzer, Kathy, 96
Syedikh, Yuriy, 96
Szewinska, Irena Kirszenstein, 96
Tewanima, Lou, 97
Thompson, Daley, 98
Thorpe, Jim, 98
Toomey, Bill, 99
Toussaint, Cheryl, 99
Tyus, Wyomia, 100-101
van Wolvelaere, Patty, 102
Viren, Lasse, 102
Waitz, Grete Andersen, 103
Walker, John, 104
Walsh, Stella, 104
Warmerdam, Cornelius, 105
White, Willye, 107
Wottle, Dave, 109
Wright, Thelma, 109

Young, Candy, 109
Zatopek, Emil, 110
Zybina, Galina, 110

Volleyball

Peppler, Mary Jo, 78

Wrestling

Albano, Captain Lou, 3
André the Giant, 5
Animal, The, 5
Atlas, Tony, 6
Backlund, Bob, 6
Berlenbach, Paul, 10
Big John Studd, 11
Blackwell, Jerry, 11
Body, The, 12
Brody, Bruiser, 15
Bundy, King Kong, 16
Cornette, Jim, 23
Dragon, 29
Gable, Dan, 35
Gagne, Greg, 35
Garvin, Jim, 35
Hall, Scott, 41
Hammer, The, 41
Hansen, Stan, 42
Hillbilly Jim, 45
Hogan, Hulk, 46
Iron Sheik, The, 48
Jack, Billy, 49
Junkyard Dog, 52
Lady Maxine, 56

Lugar, Lex, 61
Macho Man, 63
McMahon, Vince Jr., 64
Magnum, T. A., 64
Martel, Rick, 66
Mascaras, Mil, 66
Million Dollar Man, 69
Missing Link, 69
Mr. Wonderful, 69
Moolah, 70
Muraco, Magnificent Don, 71
Nature Boy, 73
Patera, Ken, 77
Piper, Rowdy Roddy, 79
Red Rooster, 81
Rhodes, Dusty, 82
Richter, Wendi, 82
Roberts, Jake the Snake, 83
Rocca, Argentina, 84
Rotundo, Mike, 86
Rude, Ravishing Rick, 86
Sammartino, Bruno, 88
Santana, Tito, 88
Slaughter, Sargeant, 92
Street, Adrian, 95
Superfly, 96
Thesz, Lou, 97
Uncle Elmer, 101
Valiant, Jimmy, 101
Von Erich, David, 103
Von Erich, Kerry, 103
Von Erich, Kevin, 103
Von Raschke, Baron, 103
Windham, Barry, 108
Zbyszko, Larry, 110

129

Index to Women Sports Figures

Albright, Tenley Emma, 3
Allen, Lisa-Marie, 4
Applebee, Constance, 5
Ashford, Evelyn, 6
Austin, Tracy, 6
Babashoff, Shirley, 6
Babilonia, Tai Reina, 6
Bacon, Mary, 6
Balas, Iolanda, 7
Barron, Gayle, 7
Bartz, Jennifer, 8
Baugh, Laura Zonetta, 8
Beck, Trudy, 9
Belote, Melissa Louise, 9
Benoit, Joan, 10
Berg, Patricia Jane, 10
Berg, Sharon, 10
Bingay, Roberta Gibb, 11
Bjurstedt, Molla, 11
Blankers-Koen, Fanny, 12
Blazejowski, Carol, 12
Blumberg, Judy, 12
Boudrot, Denise, 13
Brorsen, Metha, 15
Bussey, Shelia, 16
Campbell, Robin Theresa, 17
Casals, Rosemary, 18
Chadwick, Florence May, 19
Chaffee, Suzy, 19
Cheng, Chi, 20
Chin, Tiffany, 20
Clark, Eugenie, 20
Cochran, Barbara Ann, 21
Cochran, Linda, 21
Cochran, Marilyn, 21
Collett, Glenna, 22
Comaneci, Nadia, 22
Connolly, Maureen, 22

Cooksey, Marty, 23
Court, Margaret Smith, 23
Cox, Diane, 24
Crabtree, Helen, 24
Crump, Diane, 24
Curtis, Ann, 25
Cuthbert, Betty, 25
Davison, Ann, 26
Decker, Mary, 26
DeLeeuw, Dianne, 27
De Varona, Donna, 27
Didrikson, Babe, 27-28
Drechsler, Heike Daute, 29
Earle, Sylvia, 29
Ederle, Trudy, 29
Ender, Kornelia, 30
Evert, Chris, 30
Fikotova, Olga, 31
Fleming, Peggy Gale, 32
Fraser, Dawn, 34
Fraser, Gretchen Kunigk, 34
Fratianne, Linda Sue, 34
Frederick, Jane, 34
Fuchs, Becky, 34
Fuchs, Ruth, 34
Fuller, Genia, 34
Fuller, Peggy, 34
Garner, Kati, 35
Genesko, Lynn, 36
Gibson, Althea, 36
Goolagong, Evonne, 38
Gould, Shane Elizabeth, 38
Greene, Nancy, 39
Gurney, Hilda, 40
Guthrie, Janet, 41
Hamill, Dorothy, 41
Heddy, Kathy, 43
Heiden, Beth, 44

Heiss, Carol, 44
Henie, Sonja, 44
Henning, Anne, 44
Hlavaty, Jana, 45
Hotchkiss, Hazel, 46
Huntley, Joni, 48
Jackson, Nell, 49
Jacobs, Helen Hull, 49
Johnson, Dammy Williams, 50
Johnson, Gail, 50
Johnson, Kathy, 51
Johnson, Trudy, 51
Jones, Sue Sally, 52
Joyce, Joan, 52
Kazankina, Tatyana, 53
Kim, Nelli, 54
King, Billie Jean Moffitt, 54
King, Micki, 54-55
Kinmont, Jill, 55
Kirk, Tammy Jo, 55
Koch, Marita, 55
Korbut, Olga, 56
Kusner, Kathy, 56
Ladewig, Marion, 56
Lady Maxine, 56
Larrieu, Francie, 57
Lenglen, Suzanne, 58
Lombardi, Lella, 60
Loock, Christine, 60
Lopez, Nancy, 60
Lynn, Janet, 61
McCormick, Patty, 62
McCutcheon, Floretta, 62
McEvoy, Michele, 63
MacInnis, Nina, 63
McNamara, Julianne, 64
Magnussen, Karen, 64
Mann, Carol, 65
Manning, Madeline, 65
Marble, Alice, 65
Mauermayer, Gisela, 67
Mead, Andy, 68
Meyer, Debbie, 68
Miller, Kathy, 69
Moser-Proell, Annemarie, 71
Muldowney, Cha Cha, 71
Navratilova, Martina, 73
Nelson, Cindy, 73
Nyad, Diana, 74

O'Neil, Kitty Linn, 75
Parry, Zale, 77
Payne, Nancy, 77
Peck, Annie Smith, 78
Peppler, Mary Jo, 78
Phillips, Kristie, 79
Pirtle, Sue, 79
Pitou, Penny, 79
Prudom, Benjie Bell, 81
Rankin, Judy, 81
Retton, Mary Lou, 82
Richter, Wendi, 82
Rigby, Cathy, 83
Rodnina, Irina, 85
Rosendahl, Heidemarie, 85
Rubin, Barbara Jo, 86
Rudolph, Wilma, 86
Schmidt, Kathy, 89
Sears, Eleo, 90
Shank, Theresa, 90
Shea, Julie, 90
Smith, Robyn Caroline, 92
Smith, Stacy, 92
Soutar, Judy Cook, 93
Sperber, Paula, 93
Starbuck, Jo Jo, 94
Stecher, Renate Meissner, 94
Stenersen, Johanna, 94
Strickland, Shirley, 95
Switzer, Kathy, 96
Szabo, Ekaterina, 96
Szewinska, Irena Kirszenstein, 96
Taylor, Valerie, 97
Thomas, Debi, 97
Thurman, Sammy Fancher
Toussaint, Cheryl, 99
Turton, Janene, 100
Tyus, Wyomia, 100-101
van Wolvelaere, Patty, 102
Vinson-Owen, Maribel, 102
von Saltza, Chris, 103
Wade, Virginia, 103
Waitz, Grete Andersen, 103
Walsh, Stella, 104
Weld, Tee, 106
Wene, Sylvia, 106
White, Willye, 107
Whitworth, Kathy, 107
Wilkins, Debbie, 107

Wills, Helen, 108
Wright, Mickey, 109
Wright, Thelma, 109
Young, Candy, 109

Young, Sheila, 109
Zayak, Elaine, 110
Zybina, Galina, 110

Index to Sports Figures by Country of Origin

Argentina

Fangio, Juan Manuel, 31
Reutemann, Carlos, 82
Vilas, Guillermo, 102

Australia

Brabham, Jack, 13
Caldwell, John, 17
Court, Margaret Smith, 23
Cuthbert, Betty, 25
Elliott, Herbert James, 30
Fraser, Dawn, 34
Goolagong, Evonne, 38
Gould, Shane Elizabeth, 38
Hoad, Lewis, 45
Laver, Rod, 58
O'Dea, Patrick John, 74
Rosewall, Ken, 85
Strickland, Shirley, 95
Taylor, Valerie, 97
Thomson, Peter, 98

Austria

Lauda, Niki, 57
Moser-Proell, Annemarie, 71

Brazil

Fittipaldi, Emerson, 32
Pace, Carlos, 76
Pelé, 78

Canada

Apps, Syl, 5
Barkley, Doug, 7
Bathgate, Andy, 8
Beliveau, Jean Marc, 9
Berenson, Red, 10
Binkley, Les, 11
Blair, Wren, 11
Blake, Toe, 12
Bossy, Michael, 13
Bower, John William, 13
Broda, Turk, 14
Brodeur, Richard, 15
Burns, Tommy, 16
Cheevers, Gerry, 20
Ciccarelli, Dino, 20
Clarke, Bobby, 20
Cournoyer, Yvan Serge, 23
Crozier, Roger Allan, 24
Cushman, Wayne, 25
Delvecchio, Fats, 27
Dionne, Marcel, 28
Dixon, George, 28
Drayton, Jerome, 29
Dryden, Ken, 29
Durnan, Bill, 29
Esposito, Phil, 30
Esposito, Tony, 30
Ferguson, John Bowie, 31
Fleming, Reggie, 32
Geoffrion, Boom Boom, 36
Giacomin, Edward, 36
Gibson, Moon, 37
Gilbert, Gilles, 37
Gilbert, Rod, 37
Goldsworthy, Bill, 37

Green, Ted, 39
Greene, Nancy, 39
Gretsky, Wayne, 39
Hall, Glenn Henry, 41
Harper, Terry, 42
Harvey, Doug, 42
Heath, Allen, 43
Henderson, Paul Garnet, 44
Hiller, John Frederick, 45
Howe, Gordie, 47
Howe, Mark Steven, 47
Hull, Bobby, 47-48
Hull, Dennis William, 48
Imlach, Punch, 48
Jenkins, Ferguson Arthur, 49
Johnston, Eddie, 51
Kelly, Red, 53
Keon, Dave, 53
Lafleur, Guy Damien, 56
Lancaster, Ron, 57
Langford, Sam, 57
Leach, Reggie, 58   •
Lvesque, Jean-Louis, 59
Lindsay, Ted, 59
Liut, Mike, 59
Longboat, Tom, 60
Magnuson, Keith Arien, 64
Magnussen, Karen, 64
Mahovlich, Frank, 64
Martel, Rick, 66
Martin, Rick, 66
Moog, Andy, 70
Morenz, Howie, 70
Nagurski, Bronko, 72
Neilson, Jim, 73
Orr, Bobby, 75
Palmateer, Mike, 76
Parent, Bernie, 76
Park, Brad, 76
Patrick, Lester, 77
Peeters, Pete, 78
Perreault, Gil, 78
Pilote, Pierre Paul, 79
Plante, Jacques, 80
Potvin, Denis Charles, 80
Ratelle, Jean, 81
Redmond, Mickey, 81
Resch, Chico, 82
Richard, Henri, 82
Richard, Rocket, 82

Sanderson, Turk, 88
Sawchuk, Terry, 88-89
Schmidt, Milton Conrad, 89
Schultz, Dave, 89
Shore, Edward William, 91
Sittler, Darryl Glen, 92
Slocum, Joshua, 92
Smith, Billy, 92
Smythe, Conn Stafford, 92
Stasiuk, Vic, 94
Tallon, Dale, 96
Tkaczuk, Walter Robert, 99
Tremblay, J. C., 99
Trottier, Bryan, 100
Turcotte, Ron, 100
Ullman, Norman Victor, 101
Unger, Garry Douglas, 101
Van Impe, Edward Charles, 102
Voss, J.C., 103
Wakely, Ernie, 103
Worsley, Gump, 109
Wright, Thelma, 109

China

Ning, Li, 74

Cuba

Campaneris, Bert, 17
Canseco, José, 17
Carvajal, Felix, 18
Cuellar, Mike, 25
Juantorena, Alberto, 52
Oliva, Tony, 75
Perez, Tony, 78
Rojas, Cookie, 85
Salazar, Alberto, 88
Sardinias, Eligio, 88
Tiant, Luis Clemente, 98
Versalles, Zoilo, 102

Cyprus

Yepremian, Garo, 109

Czechoslovakia

Fikotova, Olga, 31
Hlavaty, Jana, 45

Mikita, Stanley, 69
Navratilova, Martina, 73
Stastny, Peter, 94
Zatopek, Emil

Denmark

Nelson, Battling, 73

Dominican Republic

Alou, Felipe Rojas, 4
Cedeno, Cesar, 19
Guerrero, Pedro, 40
Marichal, Juan Antonio, 66
Mota, Manny, 71

East Germany

Cierpinski, Waldemar, 20
Drechsler, Heike Daute, 29
Ender, Kornelia, 30
Fuchs, Ruth, 34
Koch, Marita, 55
Stecher, Renate Meissner, 94

Ethiopia

Bikila, Abebe, 11

Finland

Kolehmainen, Hannes, 55
Nurmi, Paavo Johannes, 74
Viren, Lasse, 102
Widing, Juha Markku, 107

France

André the Giant, 5
Borotra, Jean, 13
Brugnon, Jacques, 16
Cerdan, Marcel Jr., 19
Cochet, Henri, 21
Depailler, Patrick, 27
Gerbault, Alain, 36
Jarier, Jean-Pierre, 49
Killy, Jean-Claude, 54
Lacoste, Ren, 56
Laffite, Jacques, 56

Lenglen, Suzanne, 58
Levegh, Pierre, 58
Meiffret, José, 68

Great Britain

Applebee, Constance, 5
Austin, Jimmy, 6
Bannister, Roger Gilbert, 7
Blyth, Chay, 12
Campbell, Donald Malcolm, 17
Campbell, Malcolm, 17
Chichester, Francis, 20
Clark, Jim, 20
Cobb, John, 21
Coe, Sebastian, 22
Cotton, Henry, 23
Crowhurst, Donald, 24
Curry, John, 25
Davison, Ann, 26
Eyston, George Edward, 30
Fitzsimmons, Robert, 32
Guzzwell, John, 41
Hawthorn, John Michael, 43
Hill, Graham, 45
Hunt, James Simon Wallis, 48
McGregor, Rob Roy, 63
Miles, Ken, 69
Moss, Stirling Crauford, 71
Ovett, Steve, 76
Perry, Fred, 78
Piper, Rowdy Roddy, 79
Pryce, Tom, 81
Redman, Brian, 81
Rose, Alec, 85
Stewart, Jackie, 95
Street, Adrian, 95
Surtees, John, 96
Thompson, Daley, 98
Thomson, Bobby, 98
Vardon, Harry, 102
Wright, Harry, 109

Greece

Loues, Spyridon, 60
Pheidippides, 79
Seikaly, Rony, 90

Haiti

McDonald, Henry, 62

Honduras

Van Buren, Steve, 102

Hungary

Gogolak, Pete, 37

Ireland

Nash, Charlie, 72
Watson, John, 105

Italy

Andretti, Mario, 5
Ascari, Alberto, 6
Brambilla, Vittorio, 14
Carnera, Primo, 18
Chinaglia, Giorgio, 20
DePalma, Ralph, 27
Farina, Giuseppe, 31
Lombardi, Lella, 60
Merzario, Arturo, 68
Nuvolari, Tazio, 74
Pietri, Dorando, 79
Rocca, Argentina, 84
Sammartino, Bruno, 88

Japan

Gushiken, Koji, 40
Tsukahara, Mitsuo, 100

Kenya

Keino, Kip, 53

Mexico

Herrera, Efren, 45
Mascaras, Mil, 66
Ortega, Gaspar, 75
Rodriguez, Aurelio, 85
Santana, Tito, 88
Valenzuela, Fernando, 101

Monaco

Chiron, Louis Alexander, 20

Netherlands

Blankers-Koen, Fanny, 12
Blyleven, Bert, 12
Cruyff, Johan C., 24
DeLeeuw, Dianne, 27
Karsmakers, Pierre, 52
Nater, Swen, 73

New Zealand

Hulme, Denis Clive, 48
McLaren, Bruce, 64
Snell, Peter, 93
Walker, John, 104

Norway

Bjurstedt, Molla, 11
Henie, Sonja, 44
Rockne, Knute Kenneth, 85
Stenerud, Jan, 94
Waitz, Grete Andersen, 103

Panama

Brown, Panama Al, 15
Carew, Rod, 18
Sanguillen, Manny, 88

Poland

Drabowsky, Moe, 28
Marcol, Chester, 66
Walsh, Stella, 104

Puerto Rico

Cepeda, Perucho, 19
Clemente, Roberto Walker, 21
Figueroa, Ed, 31
Rodriguez, Chi-Chi, 85

Rumania

Balas, Iolanda, 7

Comaneci, Nadia, 22
Nastase, Ilie, 73
Szabo, Ekaterina, 96

Senegal

Siki, Battling, 91

South Africa

Player, Gary, 80
Scheckter, Jody, 89
Wade, Virginia, 103

Sweden

Borg, Bjorn, 13
Johansson, Ingemar, 50
Peterson, Ronnie, 78

Switzerland

Regazzoni, Clay, 82
Saudan, Sylvain, 88

Taiwan

Cheng, Chi, 20

Tanzania

Bayi, Filbert, 8

Union of Soviet Socialist Republics

Andrianov, Nikolai, 5
Brumel, Valeri, 16
Kazankina, Tatyana, 53
Kim, Nelli, 54
Korbut, Olga, 56
Rodnina, Irina, 85
Saneyev, Viktor, 88
Syedikh, Yuriy, 96
Szewinska, Irena, 96
Tretiak, Vladislav, 99
Zybina, Galina, 110

United States

Aaron, Hank, 3

Abdul-Jabbar, Kareem, 3
Abramowicz, Danny, 3
Albano, Captain Lou, 3
Albright, Tenley Emma, 3
Alexander, Pete, 3
Ali, Muhammad, 3
Allen, Dick, 4
Allen, George, 4
Allen, Lisa-Marie, 4
Allen, Marcus, 4
Allison, Bobby, 4
Almon, Bill, 4
Alston, Walter Emmons, 4
Alworth, Lance, 4
Ameche, Alan, 4
Anderson, Donny, 4
Anderson, Ken, 4
Anderson, Sparky, 4
Animal The, 5
Anson, Cap, 5
Appling, Luke, 5
Arcaro, Eddie, 5
Archibald, Nate, 5
Arfons, Art, 5
Arfons, Walt, 5
Arizin, Paul, 5
Armstrong, Henry, 6
Arnold, Billy, 6
Ashe, Arthur Robert, 6
Ashford, Emmett Littleton, 6
Ashford, Evelyn, 6
Atlas, Tony, 6
Attles, Alvin, 6
Auerbach, Red, 6
Austin, Tracy, 6
Babashoff, Shirley, 6
Babilonia, Tai Reina, 6
Backlund, Bob, 6
Bacon, Mary, 6
Baer, Max, 6
Baines, Harold D., 7
Baker, Bubba, 7
Baker, Buck, 7
Baker, Buddy, 7
Baker, Frank, 7
Baker, Terry Wayne, 7
Bando, Sal, 7
Banks, Chip, 7
Banks, Ernie, 7
Barney, Lem, 7

137

Barron, Ben, 7
Barron, Gayle, 7
Barry, Rick, 7
Bartz, Jennifer, 8
Bass, Dick, 8
Battles, Clifford Franklin, 8
Baugh, Laura Zonetta, 8
Baugh, Sammy, 8
Baughan, Maxie, 8
Baumhower, Bob, 8
Baylor, Ed, 8
Beamon, Bob, 8
Beard, Frank, 8
Bearden, Gene, 8
Beauchamp, Bobby, 8
Beban, Gary Joseph, 8
Beck, Gary, 9
Beck, Trudy, 9
Beckert, Glenn Alfred, 9
Bednarik, Chuck, 9
Belinsky, Bo, 9
Bell, Buddy, 9
Bellamy, Walt, 9
Bellino, Joe, 9
Belmont, Joe, 9
Belote, Melissa Louise, 9
Bench, Johnny Lee, 9
Bender, Charles Albert, 9
Benirschke, Rolf Joachim, 9
Benoit, Joan, 10
Berg, Moe, 10
Berg, Patricia Jane, 10
Berg, Sharon, 10
Bergey, Bill L., 10
Berlenbach, Paul, 10
Berra, Yogi, 10
Berry, Ray, 10
Bertelli, Angelo, 10
Berwanger, Jay, 10
Bettenhausen, Gary, 10
Bettenhausen, Merle, 10
Bettenhausen, Tony, 10
Bettenhausen, Tony Lee, 10
Bierman, Bernie, 11
Big John Studd, 11
Biletnikoff, Fred, 11
Bing, Dave, 11
Bingaman, Lester, 11
Bingay, Roberta Gibb, 11
Bird, Larry, 11

Birdsong, Otis, 11
Bjorkland, Garry, 11
Blackburn, Howard, 11
Blackwell, Jerry, 11
Blair, Matt, 11
Blanchard, Doc, 12
Blanda, George F., 12
Blazejowski, Carol, 12
Bleier, Rocky, 12
Blood, Johnny, 12
Blount, Melvin, 12
Blue, Vida Rochelle, 12
Blumberg, Judy, 12
Body, The, 12
Boggs, Wade Anthony, 12
Bonds, Bobby Lee, 12
Bostock, Lyman Jr., 13
Boswell, Charley, 13
Bottomley, Jim, 13
Boudrot, Denise, 13
Boyd, Oil Can, 13
Boyer, Clete, 13
Boyer, Ken, 13
Braddock, James J., 13
Bradley, Bill [basketball], 13
Bradley, Bill [football], 13
Bradshaw, Terry Paxton, 14
Brazile, Bob, 14
Breedlove, Craig, 14
Bresnahan, Duke, 14
Bressler, Rube, 14
Brett, George Howard, 14
Brickley, Charley, 14
Bridgeman, Junior, 14
Bridwell, Albert Henry, 14
Brock, Lou, 14
Brockington, John, 14
Brodie, John, 15
Brody, Bruiser, 15
Brorsen, Metha, 15
Brown, Bill, 15
Brown, Bob, 15
Brown, Fred, 15
Brown, Jim, 15
Brown, Larry, 15
Brown, Mordecai Peter, 15
Brown, Paul, 15
Brown, Pete Earlie, 15
Brown, Roger [basketball], 15
Brown, Roger [football], 15

Brown, Walter, 16
Browning, Pete, 16
Bryan, Jimmy, 16
Bryant, Bear, 16
Buckner, Quinn, 16
Budge, Don, 16
Bundy, King Kong, 16
Bunning, Jim, 16
Buoniconti, Nick, 16
Burdett, Lew, 16
Burgess, Smoky, 16
Burroughs, Jeffrey Alan, 16
Bussey, Shelia, 16
Butkus, Dick, 17
Button, Dick, 17
Butz, Dave, 17
Camp, Walter Chauncey, 17
Campanella, Roy, 17
Campbell, Earl Christian, 17
Campbell, Robin Theresa, 17
Cannon, Billy, 18
Carlos, John, 18
Carlton, Steve, 18
Carmichael, Harold, 18
Carr, Fred, 18
Carter, Don, 18
Carter, Duane, 18
Carter, Duane Jr., 18
Carter, Gary Edmund, 18
Cartwright, Alexander J., 18
Cartwright, Bill, 18
Casals, Rosemary, 18
Casper, Billy, 19
Casper, Dave, 19
Cassady, Hopalong, 19
Cauthen, Steve, 19
Chadwick, Florence May, 19
Chaffee, Suzy, 19
Chamberlain, Wilt, 19
Chamberlin, Guy, 19
Chance, Frank Leroy, 19
Charboneau, Joe, 19
Charles, Ezzard B., 19
Chase, Hal, 20
Chester, Ray, 20
Chin, Tiffany, 20
Clark, Dutch, 20
Clark, Dwight, 20
Clark, Eugenie, 20
Clarke, Fred, 21

Clemens, Roger William, 21
Cobb, Ty, 21
Cochran, Barbara Ann, 21
Cochran, Linda, 21
Cochran, Marilyn, 21
Cochran, Mickey, 21
Cochrane, Mickey, 21-22
Colavito, Rocky, 22
Colbert, Nate, 22
Collett, Glenna, 22
Collins, Doug, 22
Collins, Eddie, 22
Collins, Gary, 22
Collins, Jimmy, 22
Comiskey, Charles Albert, 22
Conerly, Charley, 22
Conner, Bart, 22
Connolly, Maureen, 22
Connors, Jimmy, 23
Cook, Greg, 23
Cooksey, Marty, 23
Cooper, Earl, 23
Corbett, Gentleman Jim, 23
Cornette, Jim, 23
Cosell, Howard Cohen, 23
Costello, Larry, 23
Cousineau, Tom, 23
Cousy, Bob, 23
Coveleski, Stanley Anthony, 23
Cowens, David William, 24
Cox, Diane, 24
Cox, Fred, 24
Crabtree, Helen, 24
Craig, Jim, 24
Cramer, Scott, 24
Crawford, Wahoo Sam, 24
Cromwell, Nolan Neil, 24
Cronin, Joe, 24
Crow, John David, 24
Crowely, Jim, 24
Crump, Diane, 24
Csonka, Larry, 24-25
Cummings, Terry, 25
Cunningham, Billy, 25
Cunningham, Glenn, 25
Curtis, Ann, 25
Curtis, Isaac, 25
Curtis, Mike, 25
Daggett, Tim, 25
Daniels, Mel, 25

139

Dantley, Adrian, 25
Darling, Ron, 25
Davis, Allen, 25
Davis, Eric, 25
Davis, Ernie, 25
Davis, Glenn, 26
Davis, Johnny, 26
Davis, Junior, 26
Dawkins, Pete, 26
Dawson, Len, 26
Day, Pea Ridge, 26
Dean, Daffy, 26
Dean, Dizzy, 26
Dean, Fred, 26
DeBusschere, Dave, 26
Decker, Mary, 26
Delahanty, Ed, 26
DeLamielleure, Joe, 27
DeMar, Clarence H., 27
Dempsey, Jack, 27
Dempsey, Tom, 27
Devaney, Bob, 27
De Varona, Donna, 27
Dickerson, Eric, 27
Dickey, Bill, 27
Didrikson, Babe, 27-28
Dierdorf, Dan, 28
Dillard, Harrison, 28
DiMaggio, Joe, 28
Dixon, Hewritt, 28
Donohue, Mark, 28
Dorsett, Tony, 28
Dragon, 29
Dressen, Charles Walter, 29
Drysdale, Don, 29
Dudley, Bill, 29
Duncan, Jim, 29
Durocher, Leo Ernest, 29
Earle, Sylvia, 29
Easley, Sonny, 29
Ederle, Trudy, 29
Ehmke, Howard John, 29
Eller, Carl Lee, 30
Ellison, Willie, 30
Erving, Julius, 30
Essegian, Chuck, 30
Evers, John Joseph, 30
Evert, Chris, 30
Fairly, Ron, 31
Farr, Mel, 31

Federspiel, Joe, 31
Feller, Bob, 31
Fencik, Gary, 31
Fidrych, Mark Steven, 31
Fingers, Rollie, 31
Finley, Chuck, 31
Fisk, Carlton Ernest, 31
Fitch, Bill, 31
Fleming, Peggy Gale, 32
Flock, Tim, 32
Flood, Curt, 32
Flowers, Tiger, 32
Floyd, Raymond, 32
Flutie, Doug, 32
Follmer, George, 32
Ford, George, 32
Ford, Phil, 32
Ford, Whitey, 32-33
Foreman, Chuck, 33
Fortmann, Danny, 33
Foster, George Arthur, 33
Foster, Rube, 33
Fouts, Dan, 33
Fowler, Bud, 33
Fox, Nellie, 33
Foxx, Jimmy, 33
Foyt, A. J., 33
Francis, Russell Ross, 33
Frank, Clinton Edward, 33
Franklin, Tony, 33
Fraser, Gretchen Kunigk, 34
Fratianne, Linda Sue, 34
Frazier, Clyde, 34
Frazier, Joe, 34
Frederick, Jane, 34
Free, World B., 34
Freehan, Bill, 34
Fregosi, Jim, 34
Friedman, Ben, 34
Frisch, Frank Francis, 34
Fuchs, Becky, 34
Fulks, Joe, 34
Fuller, Genia, 34
Fuller, Peggy, 34
Fuqua, Frenchy, 35
Gable, Dan, 35
Gabelich, Gary, 35
Gabriel, Roman, 35
Gaedel, Ed, 35
Gagne, Greg, 35

Gallagher, Alan, 35
Gans, Joe, 35
Gardner, Randy, 35
Garlits, Don, 35
Garner, Kati, 35
Garrett, Mike, 35
Garvey, Steve, 35
Garvin, Jim, 35
Gaylord, Mitch, 36
Gehrig, Lou, 36
Gehringer, Charles Leonard, 36
Geiberger, Allen, 36
Genesko, Lynn, 36
Gervin, George, 36
Giammona, Louie, 36
Gibson, Althea, 36
Gibson, Bob, 36-37
Gibson, Joshua, 37
Gilchrist, Cookie, 37
Gilliam, John Rally, 37
Gilmore, Artis, 37
Ginther, Richie, 37
Gipp, George, 37
Glidden, Bob, 37
Golden, Maverick, 37
Gomez, Lefty, 37
Gonzales, Pancho, 38
Gooden, Dwight, 38
Gordon, Al, 38
Goslin, Goose, 38
Gossage, Dick, 38
Grabarkewitz, Billy, 38
Gradisher, Randy, 38
Graham, Otto Everett Jr., 38
Graham, Robin Lee, 38
Granatelli, Andy, 38
Grange, Red, 38-39
Granger, Hoyle, 39
Grant, Bud, 39
Grant, Frank Ulysses, 39
Gray, Leon, 39
Gray, Peter, 39
Graziano, Rocky, 39
Greenberg, Hank, 39
Greene, Joe, 39
Greer, Hal, 39
Gregg, Peter, 39
Grich, Bobby, 39
Grier, Rosey, 39
Griese, Bob, 40

Griffin, Archie Mason, 40
Groat, Dick, 40
Groh, Heinie, 40
Grote, Jerry, 40
Grove, Lefty, 40
Groza, Louis Roy, 40
Guglielmo, Angelo, 40
Guidry, Ron, 40
Gurney, Dan, 40
Gurney, Hilda, 40
Guthrie, Bill, 40
Guthrie, Janet, 41
Guy, Ray, 41
Guyon, Joseph Napoleon, 41
Gwynn, Tony, 41
Hagen, Walter, 41
Halas, George, 41
Hall, Jim, 41
Hall, Scott, 41
Ham, Jack Raphael, 41
Hamill, Dorothy, 41
Hamilton, Scott, 41
Hammer, The, 41
Hannah, John Allen, 41
Hansen, Stan, 42
Harmon, Tom, 42
Harper, Tommy, 42
Harrelson, Bud, 42
Harrelson, Ken, 42
Harris, Bucky, 42
Harris, Franco, 42
Harroun, Ray, 42
Hart, Eddie, 42
Hart, Leon Joseph, 42
Hart, Marvin, 42
Hartack, Bill, 42
Hartnett, Gabby, 42
Havlicek, John, 42-43
Hawkins, Connie, 43
Hawley, Don, 43
Hayes, Bob, 43
Hayes, Elvin, 43
Hayes, Johnny, 43
Hayes, Lester, 43
Hayes, Woody, 43
Haymond, Alvin Henry, 43
Haynes, Abner, 43
Haynes, Mike, 43
Haywood, Spencer, 43
Hebner, Richard Joseph, 43

Heddy, Kathy, 43
Heffelfinger, Pudge, 44
Heiden, Beth, 44
Heiden, Eric, 44
Hein, Melvin John, 44
Heinsohn, Tom, 44
Heisman, John William, 44
Heiss, Carol, 44
Henderson, Rickey, 44
Hendricks, Ted, 44
Henning, Anne, 44
Henry, Pete, 44
Herman, Babe, 44
Hernandez, Keith, 44
Herr, Tom, 45
Herzog, Whitey, 45
Heston, Willie, 45
Heyison, Marc, 45
Hill, Calvin, 45
Hill, Philip Toll, 45
Hillbilly Jim, 45
Hinkey, Frank, 45
Hinkle, Clarke, 45
Hirsch, Crazylegs, 45
Hodges, Gil, 45
Hogan, Ben, 45-46
Hogan, Hulk, 46
Holbert, Al, 46
Holman, Nathan, 46
Holzman, Red, 46
Hooper, Harry Bartholomew, 46
Horn, Ted, 46
Hornsby, Rajah, 46
Hornung, Paul Vernon, 46
Horvath, Les, 46
Hotchkiss, Hazel, 46
Houston, Ken, 46
Howard, Elston Gene, 46
Howard, Frank Oliver, 47
Howley, Chuck, 47
Hoy, Bill, 47
Hrabosky, Al, 47
Huarte, John, 47
Hubbard, Cal, 47
Hubbell, King Carl, 47
Hubbs, Kenneth Douglass, 47
Hudson, Lou, 47
Huggins, Miller James, 47
Hundhammer, Paul, 48
Hunt, Ron, 48

Hunter, Catfish, 48
Huntley, Joni, 48
Hurtubise, Hercules, 48
Hutson, Don, 48
Insolo, Jimmy, 48
Iron Sheik, The, 48
Irvin, Monte, 48
Irwin, Hale, 49
Issel, Dan, 49
Jack, Billy, 49
Jackson, Nell, 49
Jackson, Reggie, 49
Jacobs, Helen Hull, 49
Janowicz, Vic, 49
Jarrett, Ned Miller, 49
Jefferson, John Larry, 49
Jeffries, James Jackson, 49
Jenner, Bruce, 49
Jennings, Hugh Ambrose, 49
Joersz, Eldon, 50
John, Tommy, 50
Johncock, Gordon, 50
Johnson, Barney, 50
Johnson, Big Hands, 50
Johnson, Bob, 50
Johnson, Charley, 50
Johnson, Dammy Williams, 50
Johnson, Gail, 50
Johnson, Gus, 50
Johnson, Jack, 50
Johnson, John Arthur, 50
Johnson, John Henry, 50
Johnson, Junior, 50
Johnson, Kathy, 51
Johnson, Magic, 51
Johnson, Marques, 51
Johnson, Pete, 51
Johnson, Rafer Lewis, 51
Johnson, Ron, 51
Johnson, Trudy, 51
Johnstone, Jay, 51
Jones, Alan, 51
Jones, Bert, 51
Jones, Bobby [basketball], 51
Jones, Bobby [golf], 51
Jones, Deacon, 51
Jones, Kangaroo, 51
Jones, K. C., 52
Jones, Parnelli, 52
Jones, Sam, 52

Jones, Samuel Pond, 52
Jones, Sue Sally, 52
Jordan, Lee Roy, 52
Joyce, Joan, 52
Junkyard Dog, 52
Jurgensen, Sonny, 52
Kabakoff, Harry, 52
Kaline, Al, 52
Kamm, Willie, 52
Kapp, Joe, 52
Kazmaier, Dick, 53
Keeler, Wee Willie, 53
Kell, George Clyde, 53
Kelley, John Adelbert, 53
Kelley, John J., 53
Kelley, Larry, 53
Kelly, King, 53
Kelly, Leroy, 53
Kemp, Ray, 53
Kemp, Steve, 53
Kenyon, Mel, 53
Keough, Matt, 53
Kerr, John, 54
Kiesling, Walter A., 54
Kiick, James F., 54
Killebrew, Harmon Clayton, 54
Kiner, Ralph McPherran, 54
King, Bernie, 54
King, Billie Jean Moffitt, 54
King, Dolly, 54
King, Micki, 54-55
Kingman, Dave, 55
Kinmont, Jill, 55
Kinnick, Nile Jr., 55
Kirk, Tammy Jo, 55
Kitt, Howard, 55
Kittle, Ron, 55
Klecko, Joe, 55
Klem, Bill, 55
Klosterman, Don, 55
Knievel, Evel, 55
Knight, Pete, 55
Koch, Bill, 55
Koosman, Jerry, 55
Koufax, Sandy, 56
Kramer, Jack, 56
Kramer, Jerry, 56
Kramer, Ron, 56
Kunz, George, 56
Kusner, Kathy, 56

Kwalick, Ted, 56
Ladd, Ernest, 56
Ladewig, Marion, 56
Lady Maxine, 56
Lajoie, Larry, 56
Lambeau, Curly, 57
Lambert, Jack, 57
Lamonica, Daryle Pat, 57
LaMotta, Jake, 57
Landry, Greg, 57
Landry, Tom, 57
Lane, MacArthur, 57
Langer, Jim, 57
Lanier, Bob, 57
Lanier, Willie Edward, 57
Largent, Steve M., 57
Larrieu, Francie, 57
Lattner, John Joseph, 57
Layden, Elmer F., 58
Layne, Bobby, 58
Layne, Floyd, 58
Leach, Tommy, 58
Leahy, Frank, 58
LeBaron, Edward W., 58
LeClair, Jim, 58
Lee, Bill, 58
Lee, Sammy, 58
LeFlore, Ron, 58
Lemm, Wally, 58
Lemongello, Mark, 58
Lewis, Carl, 59
Lillard, Joe, 59
Lilly, Bob, 59
Lipscomb, Gene, 59
Liston, Sonny, 59
Little, Floyd Douglas, 59
Little, Larry C., 59
Lloyd, John Henry, 59
Lobert, Hans, 59
Lockhart, Frank, 59
Lofton, James David, 59
Lolich, Mickey, 60
Lombardi, Ernie, 60
Lombardi, Vince, 60
Loock, Christine, 60
Lopez, Al, 60
Lopez, Nancy, 60
Lorenzen, Fred, 60
Loscutoff, Jim, 60
Lott, Ronnie, 60

143

Louis, Joe, 60
Love, Bob, 60
Lovellette, Clyde, 60
Lowenstein, John Lee, 61
Lucas, Jerry, 61
Lucas, John, 61
Lucas, Maurice, 61
Luciano, Ron, 61
Luckman, Sidney, 61
Lugar, Lex, 61
Lujack, John C., 61
Lunger, Brett, 61
Lurtsema, Bob, 61
Lyle, Sparky, 61
Lyman, Link, 61
Lynn, Fred, 61
Lynn, Janet, 61
McAdoo, Bob, 61-62
McAfee, George Anderson, 62
McAlister, Jim, 62
Macauley, Ed, 62
McCarthy, Joe, 62
McCarver, Tim, 62
McCluskey, Roger, 62
McCormick, Patty, 62
McCovey, Stretch, 62
McCreary, Conn, 62
McCutcheon, Floretta, 62
McDaniels, Jim, 62
McDonald, Tommy, 62
McDowell, Sam, 62
McElhenny, Hugh, 62
McElreath, Jim, 63
McEnroe, John, 63
McEvoy, Michele, 63
McEwen, Mongoose, 63
McGee, Willie, 63
McGill, Billy, 63
McGinnis, George, 63
McGinnity, Joe, 63
McGraw, Muggsy, 63
McGraw, Tug, 63
Macho Man, 63
MacInnis, Nina, 63
Mack, Connie, 63
McKay, John Harvey, 64
McKechnie, Bill, 64
Mackey, John, 64
McKinney, Steve, 64
McKoy, Wayne, 64

McLain, Denny, 64
McMahon, Vince Jr., 64
McMullen, Ken, 64
McNamara, Julianne, 64
Magerkurth, George Levi, 64
Magnum, T. A., 64
Malone, Moses, 65
Maloney, Jim, 65
Mann, Carol, 65
Manning, Archie, 65
Manning, Madeline, 65
Mantle, Mickey Charles, 65
Maranville, Rabbit, 65
Maravich, Peter Press, 65
Marble, Alice, 65
Marciano, Rocky, 65-66
Maris, Roger Eugene, 66
Marquard, Rube, 66
Marshall, Jim, 66
Marshall, Mike, 66
Martin, Billy, 66
Martin, Dugie, 66
Martin, Harvey, 66
Martin, LaRue, 66
Martin, Pepper, 66
Mathews, Eddie, 67
Mathewson, Christy, 67
Mathias, Bob, 67
Matlack, Johnny, 67
Matson, Ollie, 67
Matson, Randy, 67
Matthews, Vincent Edward, 67
Mattingly, Don, 67
Mayberry, John Claiborn, 67
Maynard, Don, 67
Mays, Carl William, 67
Mays, Rex, 68
Mays, Willie Howard, 68
Mead, Andy, 68
Mears, Rick, 68
Mears, Roger, 68
Meggyesy, Dave, 68
Melton, Bill, 68
Messing, Shep, 68
Meyer, Billy, 68
Meyer, Debbie, 68
Meyer, Louis, 68
Meyers, Chief, 68
Mikan, George Lawrence, 69
Miller, Don, 69

Miller, Johnny, 69
Miller, Kathy, 69
Million Dollar Man, 69
Mills, Billy, 69
Milton, Tommy, 69
Minton, Greg, 69
Missing Link, 69
Mr. Wonderful, 69
Mitchell, Bobby, 69
Mize, John Robert, 69
Mizell, Vinegar Bend, 69
Mizerak, Steve, 70
Molineaux, Tom, 70
Monroe, Earl, 70
Montana, Joe, 70
Montgomery, Wilbert, 70
Moolah, 70
Moore, Lenny, 70
Morcom, Boo, 70
Morgan, George T., 70
Morgan, Joe, 70
Morris, Mercury, 70
Morton, Craig L., 71
Moses, Edwin, 71
Motley, Marion, 71
Motta, Dick, 71
Mount Pleasant, Frank, 71
Muldowney, Cha Cha, 71
Mulligan, Zookeeper, 71
Mullin, Mo, 71
Munoz, Anthony, 71
Munson, Thurman Lee, 71
Muraco, Magnificent Don, 71
Murcer, Bobby Ray, 71
Murphy, Cal, 71
Murphy, Dale, 72
Murphy, Isaac, 72
Murphy, Jimmy, 72
Murphy, John Joseph, 72
Murray, Eddie Clarence, 72
Murtaugh, Dan, 72
Musial, Stan, 72
Namath, Joe, 72
Nance, Jim, 72
Nature Boy, 73
Nelsen, Bill, 73
Nelson, Cindy, 73
Nettles, Graig, 73
Nevers, Ernie, 73
Newlin, Mike, 73

Newsom, Bobo, 73
Newsome, Ozzie, 73
Nicklaus, Jack William, 73
Niekro, Phil, 73
Niland, John Hugh, 73
Nitschke, Ray, 74
Nixon, Norm Charles, 74
Nobis, Tommy, 74
Noll, Chuck, 74
Norton, Ken, 74
Nuxhall, Joe, 74
Nyad, Diana, 74
O'Brien, Davey, 74
O'Brien, Parry, 74
Odoms, Riley, 74
O'Doul, Lefty, 74
Oerter, Al, 75
O'Farrell, Bob, 75
Oldfield, Barney, 75
Oliver, Al, 75
Olsen, Merlin, 75
O'Neil, Kitty Linn, 75
Ongais, Danny, 75
Ott, Mel, 75
Ouimet, Francis, 75
Owens, Jesse, 76
Owens, Steve, 76
Page, Al, 76
Paige, Satchel, 76
Palmer, Arnold Daniel, 76
Palmer, Jim, 76
Parker, Dave, 77
Parker, Jim, 77
Parry, Zale, 77
Parsons, Johnnie, 77
Parsons, Johnny, 77
Patera, Ken, 77
Paterno, Joe, 77
Patkin, Max, 77
Patrick, Mike, 77
Patterson, Floyd, 77
Paultz, Billy, 77
Payne, Nancy, 77
Payton, Sweetness, 77
Pearson, David, 77
Pearson, Drew, 77
Peck, Annie Smith, 78
Penske, Captain, 78
Peoples, Woody, 78
Pep, Willie, 78

Peppler, Mary Jo, 78
Perkins, Don, 78
Perry, Gaylord Jackson, 78
Perry, Joe, 78
Perry, William, 78
Petrie, Geoff, 78
Petrocelli, Rico, 79
Pettit, Bob, 79
Petty, Lee, 79
Petty, Richard Lee, 79
Phillips, Kristie, 79
Phillips, Lefty, 79
Pidgeon, Harry, 79
Piersall, Jim, 79
Pirtle, Sue, 79
Pitou, Penny, 79
Plank, Eddie, 79
Plunkett, Jim, 80
Plunkett, Sherman, 80
Pollard, Art, 80
Pollard, Fritz, 80
Pont, John, 80
Porter, Kevin, 80
Posey, Sam, 80
Post, Dick, 80
Powell, Boog, 80
Powell, Marvin, 80
Prothro, Tommy, 80
Prudhomme, Snake, 81
Prudom, Benjie Bell, 81
Pruitt, Greg, 81
Puckett, Kirby, 81
Quisenberry, Dan, 81
Rader, Doug, 81
Ramsey, Frank, 81
Rankin, Judy, 81
Rashad, Ahmad, 81
Rayborn, Calvin, 81
Red Rooster, 81
Reed, Willis, 81
Reese, Pee Wee, 82
Reid, Mike, 82
Reiser, Pete, 82
Rentzel, Lance, 82
Resweber, Carroll, 82
Retton, Mary Lou, 82
Revson, Peter Jeffrey, 82
Rhodes, Dusty, 82
Rice, Jim, 82
Richter, Wendi, 82

Rickenbacker, Eddie, 83
Rickey, Branch, 83
Rigby, Cathy, 83
Riggins, John, 83
Riggs, Bobby, 83
Ripken, Cal, 83
Rivers, David, 83
Rizzuto, Phil, 83
Roberts, Fireball, 83
Roberts, Jake the Snake, 83
Roberts, Robin Evan, 83
Robertson, Isiah, 83
Robertson, Oscar Palmer, 83
Robeson, Paul LeRoy, 84
Robinson, Brooks Calbert, 84
Robinson, Dave, 84
Robinson, David Maurice, 84
Robinson, Frank, 84
Robinson, Jackie, 84
Robinson, Paul, 84
Robinson, Sugar Ray, 84
Robinson, Wilbert, 84
Rodgers, Bill, 85
Rodgers, Johnny, 85
Rogers, George Washington Jr., 85
Rose, Doug, 85
Rose, Mauri, 85
Rose, Pete, 85
Ross, Barney, 86
Rossovich, Tim, 86
Rote, Kyle Jr., 86
Roth, Joe, 86
Rotundo, Mike, 86
Roundfield, Dan, 86
Roush, Edd J., 86
Royal, Darrell K., 86
Rozelle, Pete, 86
Rozier, Mike, 86
Rubin, Barbara Jo, 86
Rude, Ravishing Rick, 86
Rudi, Joe, 86
Rudolph, Wilma, 86
Ruffin, Nate, 86
Ruland, Jeff, 87
Russell, Andy, 87
Russell, Bill, 87
Russell, Cazzie, 87
Ruth, Babe, 87
Ryan, Nolan, 87
Ryun, Jim, 87

Saberhagen, Bret William, 87
Sachs, Eddie, 87
Saddler, Sandy, 87
Sandberg, Ryne Dee, 88
Sanders, Charles A., 88
Sanders, Satch, 88
Santee, David, 88
Santee, James, 88
Santo, Ron, 88
Sarazen, Gene, 88
Sauer, George H. Jr., 88
Sayers, Gale Eugene, 89
Schaefer, Germany, 89
Schaus, Frederick, 89
Schayes, Dolph, 89
Schmidt, Kathy, 89
Schmidt, Mike, 89
Schoendienst, Red, 89
Schollander, Don, 89
Score, Herb, 89
Scott, Charlie, 89
Scott, George, 90
Scott, Jake, 90
Sears, Eleo, 90
Seaver, Tom, 90
Seibert, Michael, 90
Selmon, Lee Roy, 90
Shank, Theresa, 90
Sharkey, Jack, 90
Sharman, Bill, 90
Shaw, Wilbur, 90
Shea, Julie, 90
Shelby, Carroll, 90
Shelley, Ken, 90
Shoemaker, Willie, 90
Shorter, Frank, 91
Shula, Don, 91
Shuman, Ron, 91
Siemon, Jeff, 91
Sikma, Jack, 91
Silas, James, 91
Simmons, Al, 91
Simmons, Ted Lyle, 91
Simpson, O. J., 91
Sims, Billy, 91
Sinkwich, Frank, 91
Sisler, George Harold, 92
Skowron, Bill, 92
Slack, Mike, 92
Slaughter, Sargeant, 92

Sloan, Jerry, 92
Smith, Bruce, 92
Smith, Bubba, 92
Smith, Elmore, 92
Smith, Ozzie, 92
Smith, Robyn Caroline, 92
Smith, Stacy, 92
Snead, Sam, 92
Snell, Matt, 93
Sneva, Tom, 93
Snider, Duke, 93
Snively, Mike, 93
Snodgrass, Snow, 93
Sockalexis, Louis, 93
Soutar, Judy Cook, 93
Spahn, Warren Edward, 93
Spalding, A. G., 93
Speaker, Spoke, 93
Sperber, Paula, 93
Spitz, Mark Andrew, 93
Spock, Benjamin, 93
Spurrier, Steve, 93
Stabler, Ken Michael, 94
Stagg, Amos Alonzo, 94
Stallworth, John, 94
Stanhouse, Don, 94
Starbuck, Jo Jo, 94
Stargell, Willie, 94
Starr, Bart, 94
Staubach, Roger, 94
Stenersen, Johanna, 94
Stengel, Casey, 94-95
Still, Art, 95
Stingley, Darryl, 95
Stone, Steve, 95
Stoneham, Horace, 95
Strawberry, Darryl Eugene, 95
Strong, Ken, 95
Stuhldreher, Harry, 95
Sullivan, John Lawrence, 95
Sullivan, Pat, 95
Summers, Bob, 96
Summers, John, 96
Sunday, Billy, 96
Superfly, 96
Sutter, Bruce, 96
Swann, Lynn Curtis, 96
Switzer, Kathy, 96
Talbert, Billy, 96
Tanner, Sammy, 96

Tarkenton, Fran, 96
Tatum, Jack, 96
Taylor, Bruce Lawrence, 97
Taylor, Charles R., 97
Taylor, Jim, 97
Taylor, Larry, 97
Taylor, Lee, 97
Taylor, Otis, 97
Tekulve, Ken, 97
Tenace, Gene, 97
Terry, Bill, 97
Testaverde, Vinny, 97
Tewanima, Lou, 97
Theismann, Joe, 97
Thesz, Lou, 97
Thomas, Debi, 97
Thomas, Duane, 97
Thomas, Gorman, 98
Thomas, Pat Calvin, 98
Thompson, Dannie, 98
Thompson, David, 98
Thompson, Mickey, 98
Thomson, Johnny, 98
Thorpe, Jim, 98
Throneberry, Marvin Eugene, 98
Thurman, Sammy Fancher, 98
Thurmond, Nate, 98
Tickner, Charles, 98
Tilden, Bill, 99
Tinker, Joe, 99
Tittle, Y. A., 99
Toomey, Bill, 99
Toporcer, Specs, 99
Torre, Joe, 99
Toussaint, Cheryl, 99
Trafton, George, 99
Traynor, Pie, 99
Trevino, Lee Buck, 100
Triplett, Ernie, 100
Trippi, Charles Louis, 100
Trost, Al, 100
Tucker, Bob, 100
Tunnell, Emlen, 100
Tunney, Gene, 100
Turley, Bob, 100
Turner, Bulldog, 100
Turner, Pops, 100
Turton, Janene, 100
Tyson, Mike, 100
Tyus, Wyomia, 100-101

Uecker, Bob, 101
Uncle Elmer, 101
Unitas, Johnny, 101
Unseld, Westley, 101
Unser, Al, 101
Unser, Bobby, 101
Unser, Delbert B., 101
Upshaw, Gene, 101
Valiant, Jimmy, 101
Van Brocklin, Norm, 102
Vance, Dazzy, 102
van Wolvelaere, Patty, 102
Veeck, Bill, 102
Venturi, Ken, 102
Vessels, Billy Dale, 102
Vidmar, Peter, 102
Vingo, Carmine, 102
Vinson-Owen, Maribel, 102
Von Erich, David, 103
Von Erich, Kevin, 103
Von Erich, Kerry, 103
Von Raschke, Baron, 103
Von Saltza, Chris, 103
Vukovich, Bill, 103
Vukovich, Billy, 103
Waddell, Rube, 103
Wagner, Honus, 103
Walcott, Jersey Joe, 104
Walk, Neal Eugene, 104
Walker, Doak, 104
Walker, Herschel, 104
Walker, Jimmy, 104
Walker, Moses Fleetwood, 104
Walker, Wayne, 104
Walker, Weldy Wilberforce, 104
Walker, Wesley Darcel, 104
Wallace, Cookie, 104
Walls, Everson Collins, 104
Walton, Bill, 104
Waltrip, Darrell, 104
Wambsganss, Bill, 105
Waner, Lloyd James, 105
Waner, Paul Glee, 105
Ward, Monte, 105
Ward, Rodger, 105
Warfield, Paul D., 105
Warmerdam, Cornelius, 105
Warner, Pop, 105
Washington, Gene Alden, 105
Waterfield, Bob, 105

Watson, Tom, 105
Weatherly, Little Joe, 105
Weaver, Earl Sidney, 105
Webb, Spud, 105
Weber, Dick, 106
Webster, Mike, 106
Weiskopf, Tom, 106
Weissmuller, Johnny, 106
Weld, Tee, 106
Wene, Sylvia, 106
West, Jerry, 106
Westphal, Paul, 106
White, Bill, 106
White, Charles Raymond, 106
White, Danny, 106
White, Jo Jo, 106
White, Randy Lee, 106
White, Roy Hilton, 106
White, Stan, 106
White, Whizzer, 106
White, Willye, 107
Whitworth, Kathy, 107
Wiley, Gene, 107
Wilhelm, Hoyt, 107
Wilkens, Lenny, 107
Wilkins, Alonzo, 107
Wilkins, Debbie, 107
Wilkinson, Bud, 107
Willard, Jess, 107
Willard, Ken, 107
Williams, Billy Leo, 107
Williams, Buck, 107
Williams, Dick, 107
Williams, Joe, 107
Williams, Ted, 107-108
Wills, Helen, 108
Wills, Maury, 108
Wilson, Hack, 108
Wilson, Larry, 108
Windham, Barry, 108
Winfield, Dave, 108
Winslow, Kellen, 108
Witte, Luke, 108
Wood, Smokey Joe, 108

Wooden, John R., 108
Worthington, Red, 109
Wottle, Dave, 109
Wright, Mickey, 109
Yarborough, Cale, 109
Yarbrough, Lee Roy, 109
Yastrzemski, Carl Michael, 109
Yost, Fielding Harris, 109
Young, Candy, 109
Young, Cy, 109
Young, Sheila, 109
Young, Wilbur, 110
Yount, Robin R., 110
Zale, Tony, 110
Zayak, Elaine, 110
Zbyszko, Larry, 110
Zorn, Jim, 110

Venezuela

Aparicio, Luis Ernesto, 5
Concepcion, David Ismael, 22
Gutierrez, Coco, 41

Virgin Islands

Griffith, Emile Alphonse, 40
Jackson, Peter, 49

West Germany

Beckenbauer, Franz, 9
Becker, Boris, 9
Caracciola, Rudolf, 18
Mass, Jochen, 67
Mauermayer, Gisela, 67
Rindt, Karl-Jochen, 83
Rosendahl, Heidemarie, 85
Schmeling, Max, 89
Stuck, Hans Joachim, 95
Von der Ahe, Chris, 103

Yugoslavia

Roth, Werner, 86

Bibliography and Book Codes

Note: Listings which are followed in bold type by **CC** [Children's Catalog], **ESLC** [Elementary School Library Collection], **JHSLC** [Junior High School Library Catalog], **PLC** [Public Library Catalog], and **SHSLC** [Senior High School Library Catalog] refer to titles librarians recommend having in library collections.

AHRK   *All the Home Run Kings,* by Arthur Daley. New York: G. P. Putnam's Sons, 1972.

AMOS   *American Olympic Stars,* by Dick O'Connor. New York: G. P. Putnam's Sons, 1976.

ANFL   *All-Stars of the NFL,* by Bob Rubin. New York: Random House, 1976. **ESLC**

AOGL   *After Olympic Glory: The Lives of Ten Outstanding Medalists,* by Larry Borstein. New York: Frederick Warne, 1978. **JHSLC**

ARCD   *American Race Car Drivers,* by Mark Dillon. Minneapolis: Lerner Publications, 1974.

ARYL   *Auto Racing's Young Lions,* by Ross R. Olney. New York: G. P. Putnam's Sons, 1977. **ESLC, JHSLC**

ASHT   *American Sports Heroes of Today,* by Fred Katz. New York: Random House, 1970. **JHSLC**

AWIS   *American Women in Sports,* by Phyllis Hollander. New York: Grosset & Dunlap, 1972. **JHSLC**

BABM   *Baseball's Brilliant Managers,* by Nathan Aaseng. Minneapolis: Lerner Publications, 1982. **JHSLC**

BAPH   *Baseball's Power Hitters,* by Nathan Aaseng. Minneapolis: Lerner Publications, 1983. **JHSLC** *j 796.323* BAPP   *Basketball's Power Players,* by Nathan Aaseng. Minneapolis: Lerner Publications, 1985.

BARP   *Baseball's Ace Relief Pitchers,* by Nathan Aaseng. Minneapolis: Lerner Publications, 1984. **JHSLC**

BASS   *Baseball Superstars,* by Mike Herbert. Chicago: Childrens Press, 1986. *j 927.96 TEC*

796.357 BATA   *Baseball's All-Time All-Stars,* by Jim Murphy. New York: Clarion Books, 1984.

927.96 / 8127b BBGM   *Basketball's Big Men,* by Richard Rainbolt. Minneapolis: Lerner Publications, 1975.

j 927.96 BCHP   *Baseball's Champion Pitchers: The Cy Young Award Winners,* by Hal Butler. New York: Julian Messner, 1975.

796. B456 BEYD   *Beyond the Dream: Occasional Heroes of Sports,* by Ira Berkow. New York: Atheneum, 1975.

j 796.357 BFAM   *Baseball's Hall of Fame,* by Harvey Frommer. New York: Franklin Watts, 1985. **JHSLC**

927.96 also STO BFIP   *Baseball's Finest Pitchers,* by Nathan Aaseng. Minneapolis: Lerner Publications, 1980. *2 c*

96.357092 =92b BGMA   *Baseball's Great Managers,* by Harvey Frommer. New York: Franklin Watts, 1985.

927.96 (STO) BGSL   *Baseball's Greatest Sluggers,* by Bill Libby. New York: Random House, 1973. **CC**

927.9683 BHCF   *Boxing's Heavyweight Championship Fight,* by Julian May. Mankato, MN: Creative Education, 1976.

BHFL   *Basketball's High Flyers,* by Nathan Aaseng. Minneapolis: Lerner Publications, 1980. **ESLC**

96.357 98b BHNS   *Baseball's Hot New Stars,* by Bill Gutman. New York: Pocket Books, 1988.

796.357 BHOT   *Baseball's Hottest Hitters,* by Nathan Aaseng. Minneapolis: Lerner Publications, 1983. **JHSLC** *j 927.96* BHRH — *Baseball's Home-Run Hitters,* by Richard Rainbolt. Minneapolis: Lerner Publications, 1977.

927.96
R137 b0 BHWC — *Boxing's Heavyweight Champions,* by Richard Rainbolt. Minneapolis: Lerner Publications, 1981.

j 927.96 (STO) BIBA — *The Best in Baseball,* by Robert H. Shoemaker. Third edition revised. New York: Thomas Y. Crowell, 1974. *4c.*

j 927.96
(STO) BLPC — *Big League Pitchers and Catchers,* edited with commentary by Bennett Wayne. Champaign, IL: Garrard Publishing, 1974. *2 c*

j 927.96 BMVP — *Baseball's Most Valuable Players,* by Hal Butler. New York: Julian Messner, 1977.

BOBG — *The Book of Baseball Greats,* by S. H. Burchard. New York: Harcourt Brace Jovanovich, 1983.

j 796.323 BPLM — *Basketball's Playmakers,* by Nathan Aaseng. Minneapolis: Lerner Publications, 1983.

796.357
G 95b BPTH — *Basepaths: From the Minor Leagues to the Majors and Beyond,* by Marc Gunther. New York: Charles Scribner's Sons, 1984.

927.96
L 89b
also j 927.9
also j 927.9 (STO) BRIN — *Breaking In: Nine First-Person Accounts About Becoming an Athlete,* compiled and edited by Lawrence T. Lorimer. New York: Random House, 1974. **CC** *5c*

BSHP — *Basketball's Sharpshooters,* by Nathan Aaseng. Minneapolis: Lerner Publications, 1983.

j 927. 96 BSTG — *Basketball Superstars: Three Great Pros,* by Les Etter.
also j 927.96 (STO) Champaign, IL: Garrard Publishing, 1974. **ESLC** *3c.*

BTPL — *Behind the Plate: Three Great Catchers,* by Guernsey Van Riper, Jr. Illustrated by Jack Hearne. Champaign, IL: Garrard Publishing, 1973.

BWPL — *Baseball's Wacky Players,* by George Sullivan. New York: Dodd, Mead, 1984. **CC, JHC**

j 927.96 BZAN — *Baseball's Zaniest Stars,* by Howard Liss. New York: Random House, 1971. *2c*
927.96
L 69b (STO)

152

CACH — *The Catchers,* by Anthony Tuttle. Mankato, MN: Creative Education, 1976.

CAPS — *The Captains,* by Jack Clary. New York: Atheneum, 1978.

CBHA — *Challenged by Handicap: Adventures in Courage,* by Richard B. Lyttle. Chicago: Reilly & Lee Books, 1971. **CC, ESLC**

CENT — *The Centers,* by Robert Armstrong. Mankato, MN: Creative Education, 1977.

CHAB — *Champions at Bat: Three Power Hitters,* by Ann Finlayson. Illustrated by Paul Frame. Champaign, IL: Garrard Publishing, 1970. **ESLC**

CHCH — *Champs and Chumps: An Insider's Look at America's Sports Heroes,* by Glenn Dickey. San Francisco: Chronicle Books, 1976.

CHMP — *The Champions* by Bernard Garfinkel. Illustrations by David K. Stone. Photographs by Dan Baliotti. New York: Platt & Munk, 1972.

CHOS — *Champions of Sports: Adventures in Courage,* by George Vass. Chicago, Reilly & Lee Books, 1970. **ESLC**

CHSP — *Champions at Speed,* by Richard Corson. New York: Dodd, Mead, 1979. **ESLC**

CIND — *Champions of the Indianapolis 500: The Men Who Have Won More Than Once,* by Bill Libby. New York: Dodd, Mead, 1976.

COAA — *The Coaches,* by Robert Armstrong. Mankato, MN: Creative Education, 1977.

COAH — *The Coaches,* by Sam Hasegawa. Photos by Vernon J. Biever and John E. Biever. Mankato, MN: Creative Education, 1975.

COAL — *The Coaches,* by Bill Libby. Chicago: Henry Regnery, 1972.

CSPS — *Comeback Stars of Pro Sports,* by Nathan Aaseng. Minneapolis: Lerner Publications, 1983.

CTTC — *Champions of the Tennis Court,* by Hal Higdon. Englewood Cliffs, NJ: Prentice-Hall, 1971.

153

CWSP   *Contributions of Women: Sports,* by Joan Ryan. Minneapolis: Dillon Press, 1975. **ESLC, JHSLC**

DANF   *Dan Fouts, Ken Anderson, Joe Theismann, and Other All-Time Great Quarterbacks,* edited by Phyllis and Zander Hollander. New York: Random House, 1983. **JHSLC**

DEFL   *The Defensive Linemen,* by Jay H. Smith. Photos by Vernon J. Biever and John E. Biever. Mankato, MN: Creative Education, 1975.

DOSW   *Drama on the Speedway,* by Ross R. Olney. New York: Lothrop, Lee & Shepard, 1978. **ESLC**

DRID   *Dreams into Deeds: Nine Women Who Dared,* by Linda Peavy and Ursula Smith. New York: Charles Scribner's Sons, 1985. **JHSLC**

DTDD   *Dirt Track Daredevils,* by Joe Scalzo. New York: Grosset & Dunlap, 1975.

FATP   *Famous Tennis Players,* by Trent Frayne. New York: Dodd, Mead, 1977. **JHSLC**

FBAB   *Football's Breakaway Backs,* by Nathan Aaseng. Minneapolis: Lerner Publications, 1980.

FBRN   *Football Running Backs: Three Ground Gainers,* by David R. Collins. Champaign, IL: Garrard Publishing, 1976. **ESLC**

FCBL   *Football's Crushing Blockers,* by Nathan Aaseng. Minneapolis: Lerner Publications, 1982. **JHSLC**

FCQB   *Football's Clever Quarterbacks,* by Richard Rainbolt. Minneapolis: Lerner Publications, 1975.

FDDB   *Football's Daring Defensive Backs,* by Nathan Aaseng. Minneapolis: Lerner Publications, 1984.

FHHL   *Football's Hard-Hitting Linebackers,* by Nathan Aaseng. Minneapolis: Lerner Publications, 1984.

FHPL   *Famous Hockey Players,* by Trent Frayne. New York: Dodd, Mead, 1973. **CC, JHSLC**

FMAW   *Famous Modern American Women Athletes,* by Helen Hull Jacobs. New York: Dodd, Mead, 1975. **JHSLC**

FOCC   *Football's Cunning Coaches,* by Nathan Aaseng. Minneapolis: Lerner Publications, 1981.

FOIB   *Football's Incredible Bulks,* by Nathan Aaseng. Minneapolis: Lerner Publications, 1987.

FORW   *The Forwards,* by Robert Armstrong. Mankato, MN: Creative Education, 1977.

FPBS   *Famous Pro Basketball Stars,* by William Heuman. New York: Dodd, Mead, 1970. **ESLC, JHSLC**

FPPR   *Football's Punishing Pass Rushers,* by Nathan Aaseng. Minneapolis: Lerner Publications, 1984.

FRRB   *Football's Rugged Running Backs,* by Richard Rainbolt. Minneapolis: Lerner Publications0, 1975.

FSHR   *Football's Sure-Handed Receivers,* by Nathan Aaseng. Minneapolis: Lerner Publications, 1980.

FSSS   *Football Superstars of the '70s,* by Bill Gutman. New York: Julian Messner, 1975. **ESLC, JHSLC**

FSTK   *Football's Steadiest Kickers,* by Nathan Aaseng. Minneapolis: Lerner Publications, 1981.

FSWS   *Four Stars from the World of Sports,* by Clare and Frank Gault. Drawings by Ted Burwell. New York: Walker, 1973.

FTTE   *Football's Toughest Tight Ends,* by Nathan Aaseng. Minneapolis: Lerner Publications, 1981.

FWQB   *Football's Winning Quarterbacks,* by Nathan Aaseng. Minneapolis: Lerner Publications, 1980.

FWTP   *Famous Women Tennis Players,* by Trent Frayne. New York: Dodd, Mead, 1979.

GAML   *The Greatest American Leaguers,* by Al Hirshberg. New York: G. P. Putnam's Sons, 1970. **ESLC**

GARD   *Great American Race Drivers,* by Bill Libby. New York: Cowles, 1970.

GBST   *Great Baseball Stories: Today and Yesterday,* by Bill Gutman. New York: Julian Messner, 1978.

GCEN   *The Great Centers,* by Ian Thorne. Mankato, MN: Creative Education, 1976.

GCIS   *Great Comebacks in Sports,* by Phil Pepe. New York: Hawthorn Books, 1975.

GCML   *Great Catchers in the Major Leagues,* by Jack Zanger. New York: Random House, 1970. **ESLC**

GCPB   *Great Centers of Pro Basketball,* by Bob Rubin. New York: Random House, 1975.

GDEF   *The Great Defensemen,* by Ian Thorne. Mankato, MN: Creative Education, 1976.

GDGR   *Great Drivers, Great Races,* by Howard Liss. Philadelphia: J. B. Lippincott, 1973.

GFAW   *Games of Fear and Winning: Sports with an Inside View,* by Jack Ludwig. New York: Doubleday, 1976.

GGPH   *Great Goalies of Pro Hockey,* by Frank Orr. New York: Random House, 1973.

GIFC   *Gifford on Courage,* by Frank Gifford with Charles Mangel. New York: M. Evans, 1976.

GIML   *Great Infielders of the Major Leagues,* by Dave Klein. New York: Random House, 1972.

GIND   *Go, Indians! Stories of the Great Indian Athletes of the Carlisle School,* by Moss Hall. Los Angeles: Ward Ritchie Press, 1971. **ESLC**

GISP   *The Greatest in Sports: All Time Heroes of Baseball, Football & Track,* by Mac Davis. Illustrated by Sam Nisenson. New York: World, 1972.

GLBN   *Great Linebackers of the NFL,* by Richard Kaplan. New York: Random House, 1970.

GLSF *Great Latin Sports Figures: The Proud People,* by Jerry Izenberg. New York: Doubleday, 1976. **ESLC**

GLTR *Glorious Triumphs: Athletes Who Conquered Adversity,* by Vernon Pizer. Revised edition. New York: Dodd, Mead, 1980. **SHSLC**

GMIN *Great Moments in the Indy 500,* by Edward F. Dolan, Jr. New York: Franklin Watts, 1982.

GNFL *Gamebreakers of the NFL,* by Bill Gutman. New York: Random House, 1973.

GOAL *The Great Goalies,* by Ian Thorne. Mankato, MN: Creative Education, 1976.

GOGR *Golfing Greats: Two Top Pros,* by Guernsey Van Riper, Jr. Champaign, IL: Garrard Publishing, 1975. **ESLC**

GOLF *The Great Golfers,* by Rex Lardner. New York: G. P. Putnam's Sons, 1970. **JHSLC**

GOLG *Golden Girls: True Stories of Olympic Women Stars,* by Carli Laklan. New York: McGraw-Hill, 1980.

GOTT *The Glory of Their Times: The Story of the Early Days of Baseball Told by the Men Who Played It,* by Lawrence S. Ritter. New enlarged edition. New York: William Morrow, 1984. **PLC, SHSLC**

GPCP *Great Pass Catchers in Pro Football,* by Howard Coan. New York: Julian Messner, 1971. **ESLC, JHSLC**

GPQU *Great Pro Quarterbacks,* by The New York Times Sports Staff. Edited by Lud Duroska. New York: Grosset & Dunlap, 1972. **ESLC, JHSLC**

GPRB *Great Pro Running Backs,* by The New York Times Sports Staff. Edited by Lud Duroska. New York: Grosset & Dunlap, 1973. **JHSLC**

GRBF *Great Running Backs in Pro Football,* by Phil Berger. New York: Julian Messner, 1970. **ESLC**

GRLS *Great Lives: Sports,* by George Sullivan. New York: Charles Scribner's Sons, 1988.

GRUN *The Great Running Backs,* by George Sullivan. New York: G. P. Putnam's Sons, 1972. **PLC**

GSTN *Greatest Stars of the NBA,* by Phil Pepe. Englewood Cliffs, NJ: Prentice-Hall, 1970. **SHSLC**

GTGO *Golf: The Great Ones,* by Michael McDonnell. New York: Drake Publishers, 1973.

GUAR *The Guards,* by Robert Armstrong. Mankato, MN: Creative Education, 1977.

GWNG *The Great Wingmen,* by Ian Thorne. Mankato, MN: Creative Education, 1976.

HATG *Heismen: After the Glory,* by Dave Newhouse. St. Louis, MO: Sporting News, 1985. **PLC**

HEIS *Heroes of the Heisman Trophy,* by Bill Libby. New York: Hawthorn Books, 1973. **JHSLC**

HFGO *Hockey's Fearless Goalies,* by Nathan Aaseng. Minneapolis: Lerner Publications, 1984. **CC**

HGAS *Hockey's Greatest All-Stars,* by Howard Liss. New York: Hawthorn Books, 1972.

HGST *Hockey's Greatest Stars,* by Frank Orr. New York: G. P. Putnam's Sons, 1970. **ESLC, JHSLC**

HHCR *Heroes of the Hot Corner: Great Third Basemen of the Major Leagues,* by Bill Libby. New York: Franklin Watts, 1972.

HHOT *Hockey Hotshots,* edited with commentary by Bennett Wayne. Champaign, IL: Garrard Publishing, 1977.

HITT *The Hitters,* by Thomas Braun. Mankato, MN: Creative Education, 1976.

HMKM *Hockey's Masked Men: Three Great Goalies,* by Les Etter. Illustrated by Larry Noble. Champaign, IL: Garrard Publishing, 1976.

HOFB *Hall of Fame Baseball,* by Mac Davis. Cleveland, OH: Collins-World, 1975.

HOHR   *Heroes of the Home Run,* edited with commentary by Bennett Wayne. Champaign, IL: Garrard Publishing, 1973.

HOPH   *Heroes of Pro Hockey,* by Stan Fischler. New York: Random House, 1971.

HOSS   *Hockey's Super Scorers,* by Nathan Aaseng. Minneapolis: Lerner Publications, 1984.

HROS   *Heroes of Soccer,* by Larry Adler. New York: Julian Messner, 1980.

HSCR   *Heroes of Stock Car Racing,* by Bill Libby. New York: Random House, 1975. **ESLC**

HSPB   *Hot Shots of Pro Basketball,* by Lou Sabin. New York: Random House, 1974.

HSPH   *Hot Shots of Pro Hockey,* by Walt MacPeek. New York: Random House, 1975.

HSSE   *Hockey Stars of the 70s,* by Frank Orr. New York: G. P. Putnam's Sons, 1973.

HTSC   *Hockey's Top Scorers,* by Richard Rainbolt. Minneapolis: Lerner Publications, 1981.

HUNB   *100 Greatest Baseball Heroes,* by Mac Davis. New York: Grosset & Dunlap, 1974.

HUNF   *100 Greatest Football Heroes,* by Mac Davis. New York: Grosset & Dunlap, 1973. **JHSLC**

HUNW   *100 Greatest Women in Sports,* by Phylllis Hollander. New York: Grosset & Dunlap, 1976. **JHSLC**

HWCH   *The Heavyweight Champions,* by John Durant. Sixth edition revised and enlarged. New York: Hastings House, 1976. **JHSLC, PLC**

INFD   *The Infielders,* by Jay H. Smith. Mankato, MN: Creative Education, 1976.

IRCD   *International Race Car Drivers,* by Mark Dillon and Frank Haigh. Minneapolis: Lerner Publications, 1974.

KOMS   *Kings of Motor Speed,* by Ross R. Olney. New York: G. P. Putnam's Sons, 1970. **JHSLC**

KOTR   *Kings of the Rink,* by Stan Fischler. New York: Dodd, Mead, 1978. **JHSLC**

LGPS   *Little Giants of Pro Sports,* by Nathan Aaseng. Minneapolis: Lerner Publications, 1980. **ESLC**

LINE   *The Linebackers,* by Sam Hasegawa. Photos by Vernon J. Biever and John E. Biever. Mankato, MN: Creative Education, 1975.

LONH   *The Lonely Heroes: Professional Basketball's Great Centers,* by Merv Harris. New York: Viking Press, 1975.

MANG   *The Managers,* by Jay H. Smith. Mankato, MN: Creative Education, 1976.

MARA   *The Marathoners,* by Hal Higdon. New York: G. P. Putnam's Sons, 1980.

MARS   *Modern Auto Racing Superstars,* by Ross R. Olney. New York: Dodd, Mead, 1978.

MASK   *The Masked Marvels: Baseball's Great Catchers,* edited by Phyllis and Zander Hollander. New York: Random House, 1982.

MBBS   *Modern Basketball Superstars,* by Bill Gutman. New York: Dodd, Mead, 1975.

MDRS   *Modern Drag Racing Superstars,* by Ross R. Olney. New York: Dodd, Mead, 1981.

MHSS   *Modern Hockey Superstars,* by Bill Gutman. New York: Dodd, Mead, 1976.

MITN   *The Men in the Nets,* by Jim Hunt. Revised edition. New York: McGraw-Hill Ryerson, 1972. ESLC

MLRG   *Mary Lou Retton and the New Gymnasts,* by Herma Silverstein. New York: Franklin Watts, 1985.

MMWS   *More Modern Women Superstars,* by Bill Gutman. New York: Dodd, Mead, 1979. **JHSLC**

MOBS   *Modern Baseball Stories,* by Bill Gutman. New York: Dodd, Mead, 1973.

MOSS   *Modern Olympic Superstars,* by George Sullivan. New York: Dodd, Mead, 1979.

MSLB   *Men of the Seventies: The Linebackers,* by Rick Smith. New York: National Football League, 1976.

MSRS   *Modern Speed Record Superstars,* by Ross R. Olney. New York: Dodd, Mead, 1982. **ESLC, JHSLC**

MSSS   *Modern Soccer Superstars,* by Bill Gutman. New York: Dodd, Mead, 1979.

MWSS   *Modern Women Superstars,* by Bill Gutman. New York: Dodd, Mead, 1977. **ESLC, JHSLC**

NFLS   *NFL Superstars,* by Hal Lundgren. Chicago: Childrens Press, 1983. **JHSLC**

OTWU   *On the Way Up: What It's Like in the Minor Leagues,* by Dave Klein. New York: Julian Messner, 1977. **ESLC**

PBBM   *Pro Basketball's Big Men,* by Dave Klein. New York: Random House, 1973. **ESLC**

PBGR   *Pro Basketball's Greatest: Selected All-Star Offensive and Defensive Teams,* by Louis Sabin. New York: G. P. Putnam's Sons, 1976. **ESLC**

PFHT   *Pro Football Heroes of Today,* by Berry Stainback. New York. Random House, 1973. **ESLC**

PHHT   *Pro Hockey Heroes of Today,* by Bill Libby. New York: Random House, 1974.

PIBB   *Pioneers of Baseball,* by Robert Smith. Boston: Little, Brown, 1978. **JHSLC**

POBS   *Pioneers of Black Sport,* by Ocania Chalk. New York: Dodd, Mead, 1975. **PLC, SHSLC**

PROQ   *The Pro Quarterbacks,* by Milton J. Shapiro. New York: Julian Messner, 1971. **JHSLC**

PTCH   *The Pitchers,* by Jay H. Smith. Mankato, MN: Creative Education, 1976.

QUAR   *The Quarterbacks,* by Sam Hasegawa. Photos by Vernon J. Biever and John E. Biever. Mankato, MN: Creative Education, 1975.

QOTC   *Queens of the Court,* by George Sullivan. New York: Dodd, Mead, 1974. **CC**

RACE   *Road Racers: Today's Exciting Driving Stars,* by Robert B. Jackson. New York: Henry Z. Walck, 1977. **ESLC, JHSLC**

RBML   *Record-Breakers of the Major Leagues,* by Lou Sabin. New York: Random House, 1974.

RBPS   *Record Breakers of Pro Sports,* by Nathan Aaseng. Minneapolis: Lerner Publications, 1987.

RCHN   *Remarkable Children: Twenty Who Made History,* by Dennis Brindell Fradin. Boston: Little, Brown, 1987. **JHSLC**

RECS   *The Receivers,* by Jay H. Smith. Photos by Vernon J. Biever and John E. Biever. Mankato, MN: Creative Education, 1975.

ROOK   *Rookie: The World of the NBA,* by David Klein. Chicago: Cowles, 1971.

RUNB   *The Running Backs,* by Charles and Ann Morse. Photographs by Vernon J. Biever and John E. Biever. Mankato, MN: Creative Education, 1975.

SBWL   *Super Bowl Superstars: The Most Valuable Players in the NFL's Championship Game,* by Pete Alfano. New York: Random House, 1982.

SCHA   *Super Champions of Auto Racing,* by Ross R. Olney. New York: Clarion Books, 1984. **JHSLC**

SCIH   *Super Champions of Ice Hockey,* by Ross R. Olney. New York: Clarion Books, 1982.

SFST   *Superfists,* by Graham Houston. New York: Crown, 1975.

SGBM   *Strategies of the Great Baseball Managers,* by Hank Nuwer. New York: Franklin Watts, 1988.

SGFC   *Strategies of the Great Football Coaches,* by Hank Nuwer. New York: Franklin Watts, 1988.

SHWQ   *Sports Heroes Who Wouldn't Quit,* by Hal Butler. New York: Julian Messner, 1973. **JHSLC**

SING   *The Singlehanders,* by Peter Heaton. New York: Hastings House, 1976.

SMAA   *Sport Magazine's All-Time All Stars,* edited by Tom Murray. New York: Atheneum, 1977.

SMKR   *The Speedmakers: Great Race Drivers,* by David J. Abodaher. New York: Julian Messner, 1979. **JHSLC**

SOML   *Stars of the Major Leagues,* by Dave Klein. New York: Random House, 1974.

SOPB   *Stars of Pro Basketball,* by Lou Sabin and Dave Sendler. New York: Random House, 1970. **ESLC**

SOSW   *Superstars of the Sports World,* by Bill Gutman. New York: Julian Messner, 1978. **JHSLC**

SOTO   *Stars of the Olympics,* by Bill Libby. New York: Hawthorn Books, 1975. **JHSLC**

SPIM   *The Sports Immortals,* by The Associated Press Sports Staff. Edited by Will Grimsley. Englewood Cliffs, NJ: Prentice-Hall, 1972.

SPKS   *Speed Kings: World's Fastest Humans,* by Irwin Stambler. New York: Doubleday, 1973. **JHSLC**

SPML   *Star Pitchers of the Major Leagues,* by Bill Libby. New York: Random House, 1971.

SPRN   *Star Pass Receivers of the NFL,* by John Devaney. New York: Random House, 1972. **ESLC, JHSLC**

SPSP   *Supersubs of Pro Sports,* by Nathan Aaseng. Minneapolis: Lerner Publications, 1983.

SQBN   *Star Quarterbacks of the NFL,* by Bill Libby. New York: Random House, 1970. **ESLC**

SRBN   *Star Running Backs of the NFL,* by Bill Libby. New York: Random House, 1971.

SSAR   *Superstars of Auto Racing,* by Ross R. Olney. New York: G. P. Putnam's Sons, 1975.

SSOG   *Superstars of Golf,* by Nick Seitz and Bob Toski. Norwalk, CT: Golf Digest, 1978.

STOF   *The Story of Football,* by Dave Anderson. New York William Morrow, 1985.

STOH   *The Story of Hockey,* by Frank Orr. New York: Random House, 1971.

STOI   *Stars on Ice,* by Elizabeth Van Steenwyk. New York: Dodd, Mead, 1980.

SUPC   *The Supercars and the Men Who Raced Them,* by Irwin Stambler. New York: G. P. Putnam's Sons, 1975.

SUPD   *Superdrivers: Three Auto Racing Champions,* by Bill Libby. Champaign, IL: Garrard Publishing, 1977.

SUSS   *Superstars Stopped Short,* by Nathan Aaseng. Minneapolis: Lerner Publications, 1982. **JHSLC**

SWTR   *Superstars of Women's Track,* by George Sullivan. New York: Dodd, Mead, 1981.

SXWD   *Six Who Dared,* by Sandra Gardner. New York: Julian Messner, 1981.

TDTL   *They Dared to Lead: America's Black Athletes,* edited by Phyllis and Zander Hollander. New York: Grosset & Dunlap, 1972. **JHSLC**

TENN   *Tennis: Great Stars, Great Moments,* by Andrew Lawrence. New York: G. P. Putnam's Sons, 1976. **ESLC**

TGCH   *Track's Greatest Champions,* by Cordner Nelson. Los Altos, CA: Tafnews Press, 1986.

THCH   *That Championship Feeling: The Story of the Boston Celtics,* by Joe Fitzgerald. New York: Charles Scribner's Sons, 1975.

THSA   *They Sailed Alone: The Story of the Single-Handers,* by MacDonald Harris. Boston: Houghton Mifflin, 1972.

TRGW   *Track's Greatest Women,* by Jon Hendershott. Los Altos, CA: Tafnews Press, 1987.

TRMM   *Track's Magnificent Milers,* by Nathan Aaseng. Minneapolis: Lerner Publications, 1981.

TSBG   *Tom Seaver's All-Time Baseball Greats,* by Tom Seaver and Martin Appel. New York: Julian Messner, 1984. **JHSLC, SHSLC**

TTOH   *They Triumphed Over Their Handicaps,* by Joan Harries. New York: Franklin Watts, 1981. **ESLC**

UFTM   *Up From the Minor Leagues of Hockey,* by Stan and Shirley Fischler. Chicago, IL: Cowles, 1971.

UHML   *Unsung Heroes of the Major Leagues,* by Art Berke. New York: Random House, 1976. **JHSLC**

UHPB   *Unsung Heroes of Pro Basketball,* by Raymond Hill. New York: Random House, 1973.

WATT   *Where Are They Today? Great Sports Stars of Yesteryear,* by John Devaney. New York: Crown Publishers, 1985.

WCHP   *The World Champions: Giuseppe Farina to Jackie Stewart,* by Anthony Pritchard. New York: Macmillan, 1974. **SHSLC**

WCMA   *World Class Marathoners,* by Nathan Aaseng. Minneapolis: Lerner Publications, 1982. **CC, JHSLC**

WGRD   *World's Great Race Drivers,* by Frank Orr. New York: Random House, 1972. **ESLC**

WHET   *Winners of the Heisman Trophy,* by John Devaney. New York: Walker, 1986. **ESLC, JHSLC**

WIGY   *Winners in Gymnastics,* by Frank Litsky. New York: Franklin Watts, 1978.

WISM   *Women in Sports: Motorcycling,* by Grace Butcher. New York: Harvey House, 1976.

WISP   *Women in Sports,* by Irwin Stambler. New York: Doubleday, 1975. ESLC, JHSLC

WISR   *Women in Sports: Rodeo,* by Elizabeth Van Steenwyk. New York: Harvey House, 1978. **JHSLC**

WISS   *Women in Sports: Skiing,* by Claire Walter. New York: Harvey House, 1977. **ESLC**

WMOT   *Winning Men of Tennis,* by Nathan Aaseng. Minneapolis: Lerner Publications, 1981. **ESLC**

WNQT   *Winners Never Quit: Athletes Who Beat the Odds,* by Nathan Aaseng. Minneapolis: Lerner Publications, 1980. **ESLC**

WNTC   *Winners on the Tennis Court,* by William G. Glickman. New York: Franklin Watts, 1978. **ESLC**

WOSS   *Winners on the Ski Slopes,* by John Fry. New York: Franklin Watts, 1979. **ESLC**

WOTI   *Winners on the Ice,* by Frank Litsky. New York: Franklin Watts, 1979. **ESLC**

WOWW   *Women Who Win,* by Florence Sabin. New York: Random House, 1975. **JHSLC, SHSLC**

WRES   *Wrestling Superstars,* by Daniel and Susan Cohen. New York: Pocket Books, 1985.

WRE2   *Wrestling Superstars II,* by Daniel and Susan Cohen. New York: Pocket Books, 1986.

WSFS   *Women in Sports: Figure Skating,* by Elizabeth Van Steenwyk. New York: Harvey House, 1976. **ESLC**

WSHR   *Women in Sports: Horseback Riding,* by Flora Golden. New York: Harvey House, 1978. **JHSLC**

WSSD   *Women in Sports: Scuba Diving,* by Hillary Hauser. New York: Harvey House, 1976.

WSTF   *Women in Sports: Track and Field,* by Diana C. Gleasner. New York: Harvey House, 1977. **ESLC, JHSLC**

WSWM   *Women in Sports: Swimming,* by Diana C. Gleasner. New York: Harvey House, 1975.

WTEN   *Women in Sports: Tennis,* by Marion Meade. New York: Harvey House, 1975.

WUND   *Winners Under 21,* edited by Phyllis and Zander Hollander. New York: Random House, 1982. **JHSLC**

WWCT   *Women Who Changed Things,* by Linda Peavy and Ursula Smith. New York: Charles Scribner's Sons, 1983. **JHSLC**

WWDA   *Women Who Dared,* by Valjean McLenighan. Illustrated by Jackie Denison. Milwaukee: Raintree Publishers, 1979. **JHSLC**

WWOS   *Wonder Women of Sports,* by Betty Millsaps Jones. New York: Random House, 1981. **ESLC**

WWOT   *Winning Women of Tennis,* by Nathan Aaseng. Minneapolis: Lerner Publications, 1981.

YANF   *Young and Famous: Sports' Newest Superstars,* by Daniel and Susan Cohen. New York: Pocket Books, 1987.